How to Manage the Perfect Factory (or) How AS6500 Can Lead to Everlasting Happiness

How to Manage the Perfect Factory (or) How AS6500 Can Lead to Everlasting Happiness

SAE INTERNATIONAL®

Warrendale, Pennsylvania, USA

400 Commonwealth Drive
Warrendale, PA 15096-0001 USA
E-mail: CustomerService@sae.org
Phone: 877-606-7323 (inside USA and Canada)
           724-776-4970 (outside USA)
FAX: 724-776-0790

Library of Congress Catalog Number 2020944259
http://dx.doi.org/10.4271/9781468601732

Information contained in this work has been obtained by SAE International from sources believed to be reliable. However, neither SAE International nor its authors guarantee the accuracy or completeness of any information published herein and neither SAE International nor its authors shall be responsible for any errors, omissions, or damages arising out of use of this information. This work is published with the understanding that SAE International and its authors are supplying information but are not attempting to render engineering or other professional services. If such services are required, the assistance of an appropriate professional should be sought.

ISBN-Print 978-1-4686-0172-5

To purchase bulk quantities, please contact: SAE Customer Service

E-mail: CustomerService@sae.org
Phone: 877-606-7323 (inside USA and Canada)
           724-776-4970 (outside USA)
Fax: 724-776-0790

Visit the SAE International Bookstore at books.sae.org

Chief Product Officer
Frank Menchaca

Publisher
Sherry Dickinson Nigam

Director of Content Management
Kelli Zilko

Production Associate
Erin Mendicino

Manufacturing Associate
Adam Goebel

contents

acknowledgements

First, my thanks and love to my wife, Kelly. When I didn't know if I should undertake this project, she encouraged me to do it. And she continues to be terrifically supportive.

And my daughters, Micah, Morgan, and Riley are all the best! Oh, yeah, and my son-in-law, Sam. He's pretty good, too.

A special thanks to my bonus daughter, E. Bronwyn Hinkle, an excellent writer herself. Check out her work on Amazon! She provided lots of "writerly" advice, guidance, and commiseration.

Thank you to the staff at SAE (especially Sherry Nigam, Becky Lemon, and Erin Mendicino) for going out on a limb and supporting this book that is somewhat of a, uh, departure from their normal publications.

And finally, to God who has blessed me beyond measure, more than I could ask or imagine.

preface

Someone should write a book about this stuff! Oh, wait, you mean me?

Well, OK. I'll do it.

But did you ever notice how most books on technical topics can be dull? Unless it's the "Star Fleet Technical Manual" or "Mr. Scott's Guide to the Enterprise," of course. No offense to all those PhDs who toiled away over their magnum opuses, hoping to bring light to the unenlightened.

So, when SAE suggested that we should have a book on Manufacturing Management, and I foolishly raised my hand to volunteer, I knew it had to be something completely different. Who wants to read a book on Manufacturing Management for fun? Who's going to curl up with a treatise on key characteristics in bed? Ok, I know there are a few of you really nerdy people out there who might, but you are the exception. Trust me.

I set out to make this book more enjoyable than educational; more fun than instructive, although you may still pick up a few tidbits of information. This is purely unintentional and any new information is included at no extra cost. Hopefully, though, this book has ended up being a little more motivational instead. Gently poking fun at the people and organizational barriers that the Manufacturing function must overcome can make those obstacles seem more surmountable. If we can laugh at them and at ourselves, maybe we can work together a little more easily.

This is all good stuff and I want you to have the confidence to know that you are doing the right things in implementing these practices.

I hope you enjoy the book and don't fall asleep!

.

CHAPTER 1

Introduction

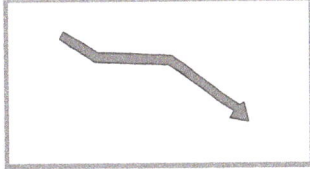

© Cartoon Resource

"This may seem counter intuitive, but maybe the solution is to lighten up."

Several years ago, I attended a conference on quality (Big Q, of course.) The opening session featured a motivational speaker of minor renown who seemed to be making the rounds of the conference circuit. After he was introduced, the house lights dimmed, the strobes flashed, and the pounding music blared. You all know the song—*Get Ready for This* (look it up on YouTube if you don't know it and prepare to be motivated.) The speaker ran up the center aisle to the podium, pumping his fists all the way. He began by leading the crowd in a chant of, "It's all about the…QUALITY!" He began the prompt, "It's all about the…" And we responded with, "QUALITY!"

From his speech that followed, he knew as much about quality as the average program manager on the street. Quality is good. And it's important. Not having quality is bad. And let's chant that mantra a few dozen more times.

I also suspect that the next day, he spoke at a convention of tax accountants, where he led them in a rousing chant of, "It's all about the…TAX DEFERRED ANNUITY INVESTMENTS!"

Other than mocking the pablum that passes for motivational speeches, my point is that the guy was right. It is really all about the QUALITY. It's the single defining and distinguishing characteristic that sticks with a customer, be it a teenager using a cell phone, a family driving a minivan, or a soldier pushing a button and hoping the rocket goes bang. In fact, I propose that the teenager, family, and soldier care much more about quality than they do about cost and schedule.

Since the SAE standard AS6500, which we will be discussing and which will bring you everlasting happiness, began with a military pedigree, let's take the soldier as an example. Does he care that the tank he is driving costs an extra $100M to develop than originally planned? Nah. That's the problem of some Lieutenant Colonel somewhere in the finance department of the Pentagon. Does he care that it got delivered six months late? Probably not too much. The old tank wasn't great, but it got along just fine. But he'll really be ticked off if the new tank stalls in the middle of downtown Islamic State of Iraq and Syria (ISIS)-city. He will curse the manufacturer of that tank until his dying day, which is hopefully, a long way off, despite stalling a lemon of a tank in downtown ISIS-city. And he will tell his family to never buy a tank from that company.

So, despite the fact that program managers agonize over cost and schedule and nag the factory guys about delivering on time and staying within budget, those things really don't matter nearly as much to the customer as quality.

What affects the quality (in this case, little Q, or rather, how well the product operates)? Quality is really a dependent variable. When designing a new product, engineers don't directly dial at a quality level. Yes, they can predict quality if they have enough data, but only based on elements of the design.

If quality is a dependent variable, what is it dependent upon? Two factors: design and manufacturing. (I bet you thought I forgot that this was supposed to be a book about manufacturing instead of quality. Or maybe you thought you misread the title of the book. "I thought it said AS6500, but maybe it was really AS9100.")

The Manufacturing Management Program (those magical words!) can impact both of the factors that contribute to quality. Manufacturing is a primary independent variable upon which quality depends. That's pretty obvious. How well the factory builds the product has a direct relationship with quality. But the Manufacturing Engineers can also influence the design to make it more productive to improve quality. So, when we say it's all about Quality, it really comes down to being all about the Manufacturing Management Program. And that's why AS6500 can lead to everlasting happiness.

A little history...

Why AS6500? Where did it come from? Why does it exist? Those are easy questions to answer. It came from the inspiration of angels and it exists to make your life, and your factory, more perfect. That's why, when you open the standard, you can still hear the faint echoes of the singing of angels.

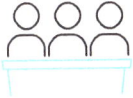 But a few more details... Gather 'round kids for an exciting bedtime story!

Once upon a time, a great big organization known as the Department of Defense actually wielded tremendous power in the marketplace. They set the standard, literally, for how to manage manufacturing and quality programs in factories. Back in the 1970s, even before disco became a thing, the wise gurus at the mighty Defense Department wrote two of the finest documents ever to grace the halls of industry: MIL-Q-9858 and MIL-STD-1528. MIL-Q, as it was affectionately known, was the standard for a Quality Management System. MIL-STD-1528 was the standard for a Manufacturing Management System. For several decades, all was well with the world. The defense industry hummed along effectively, operating to these two documents.

But then, in the mid-1990s, a dark cloud entered the realm. Evil forces sowed seeds of dissension. There was great unhappiness with military standards. The supposedly enlightened leadership at the formerly mighty Defense Department believed that these government-unique standards were driving unnecessary expenses. "If only we could do it the way that the commercial industry does things," the leaders pined. "Let us rid ourselves of these onerous standards, then the products we buy will be so much cheaper and their quality will be even better than it was before!" So, a great initiative was begun, Acquisition Reform, to eliminate those terrible standards and buy things the way that customers purchase products in the rest of society.

In 1996, the Department of Defense drove stakes into the heart of many military standards, including the venerable MIL-Q-9858 and MIL-STD-1528. With the ugly deed done, the enlightened leaders stood to survey the industry and adopt the ways of the commercial companies. From a quality perspective, ISO 9000 was immediately recognized as a replacement for MIL-Q-9858 and was adopted and placed on contract instead of MIL-Q-9858. There were some weeping and gnashing of teeth from the Quality purists, but most everyone agreed that ISO 9000 covered the important points of MIL-Q. Soon after, AS9100 arrived to enhance the quality requirements of ISO 9000 and add unique considerations for aerospace products. All was well with the world from a quality management system standpoint.

From a manufacturing management system standpoint, the story was much bleaker. Although the manufacturing management experts looked far and wide, not a replacement could be found for MIL-STD-1528. But the enlightened leaders had already moved on and claimed success, so they cared not one bit for the plight of the manufacturing function. They had no standard to turn to.

Everyone did what was right in their own eyes and chaos ensued. Programs went into production without their manufacturing processes sufficiently mature, leading to cost overruns, quality problems, late deliveries, and dogs and cats living together. The fearsome Government Accountability Office wrote report after report on the lack of manufacturing process maturity in programs and the tremendous cost and schedule impacts that resulted. The GAO complained, ironically, that the Defense Department was not developing and producing its systems the way that the commercial industry did, especially the automotive industry. The automotive manufacturers took great pains to ensure their manufacturing processes were mature, stable, and in control.

Finally, new leadership emerged at the once-again mighty Defense Department that recognized the need for a standard approach for manufacturing management. These wise leaders chose SAE International to develop and publish the new standard because SAE has so many standards that are already of a similar and related nature. Experts were gathered from across the country, both from the Defense Department and from industry to create the new document. They toiled away until the perfect product emerged from the fruit of their labors: Aerospace Standard AS6500, "Manufacturing Management Program," published in November 2014.

The rest, as they say, is history...

2

The Perfect Factory

"NEXT ON THE TOUR, OUR EMPLOYEE LOUNGE."

© Cartoon Resource

What do we mean when we say, "the perfect factory?" Oh, sure, it's probably easy to define it as something like "a company that produces products on time, on budget, and at the expected quality." But that's so pie-in-the-sky. Sure, if you follow all the practices in AS6500, that's exactly what you will achieve, and that's probably good enough for most people. But you want more. You want to exceed expectations. You want everlasting happiness. So, here is a much more idealistic description of what the perfect factory really looks like as you enter through its golden doors:

- It's sparkling clean. None of that dirt, grime, and oil from those nasty machines. No metal chips on the floor to get stuck in your shoes. Those are for other people's factories. Your factory floor (literally, the factory FLOOR) should be clean enough to eat off.

- Plenty of golf carts. The golf carts aren't necessarily for the employees, they're really for the VIP tours that you will be giving to all the important people that want to see your perfect factory. All the best factory tours I've been on have involved golf carts. Don't forget, during the tours, make as many comparisons of your company to Toyota as possible. Tell visitors that, "Our kan-ban production control system is right out of the Toyota Production System" or "We have our employees do regular morning exercises, just like Toyota." That second claim may or may not be true, but it will still impress your visitors. Anytime you can name-drop Toyota, it will reflect well on you. And maybe, just maybe, one day, Toyota will be name-dropping YOU.

- It has an in-house branch of a famous coffee shop, whose name will go without mentioning unless they provide a paid endorsement for this book. Nothing says you have a classy operation more than having "one of those" shops in your factory.

- A place for everything and everything in its place. Many factories use shadow boxes for tools and color-coded lines on the floor to outline where mobile equipment should be stored when not in use. But you can take it to the next level. We're talking shadow boxes in the cafeteria for forks, knives, spoons, napkins, and salt. And shadow boxes in the bathroom for extra rolls of toilet paper and mints. Be extremely bold and draw outlines on the floor to note where engineers and program managers are allowed to stand when they are not in their offices and are on the floor trying to "help."

- Lots of swag. Putting your company's logo on pens, water bottles, pizza cutters, socks, and toenail clippers is the best way to remind people throughout their day about what a great factory you are running.

- Classical music. This will really separate your factory from the rest of the rabble. You can pipe in some Bach, Beethoven, and Brahms, while everyone else is catering to the lowest common denominator with Van Halen, Blue Oyster Cult, and Iron Maiden.

- Posters of eagles with inspirational sayings like, "With the proper attitude, you can get the proper altitude, and soar like an eagle." These most likely do not affect morale and may even have the opposite effect, but it sends the message to visitors in your factory that you care about deep, meaningful slogans.

- Lounge and reading room. This is where employees can take a cup of that very expensive coffee from the place that will not be named and hang around and improve themselves with great literature. Be sure to scatter plenty of copies of "The Goal," "Lean Thinking," "The Machine That Changed the World," and "The Toyota Production System" around to show how enlightened your company is.

The next question you are probably asking is, "How will my success in running the perfect factory be recognized, especially outside of my company?" You probably don't care about promotions and raises; you're too high-minded for that. But it would be rewarding to get some verification from outside sources that you, in fact, run the perfect factory. Here are a few places where you might get that ego-boost:

- Continually increasing stock price
- Forbes cover story
- Harvard Business School case study on how to run the perfect factory
- Consumer Reports Best Buy recommendation for your company's product
- Amazon 5 Star reviews

On the flip side, here are some places where you don't want to be recognized:

- 60 Minutes
- Harvard Business School case study on how NOT to run a factory
- Time Magazine cover story
- Your company's product in the Dollar General bargain bin, which is especially embarrassing if you make airplanes or tanks.

3

The Manufacturing Management Program

© Cartoon Resource

What do we mean by the term "Manufacturing Management Program?" Well, I can't give away all the answers for free here. Sorry, but you're going to have to spend the additional $78.00 to order AS6500 from SAE to find that definition. After all, I get 10% of each standard sold. Oh, wait, I was told not to say that by my SAE handlers. Probably because it isn't true.

When you do spring for the $78.00, you will first ask yourself, "Why is it so expensive? It's so…short! After all, when I bought that quality standard, AS9100, it was much longer, and I felt like I got my money's worth with all of those extra requirements."

Well, despite its limited page count, you will be amazed at the font of wisdom it contains. In fact, the requirements in AS6500 are actually *better* than those in AS9100. Oh, wait, my SAE handlers told me not to say that, either. Instead, I'm supposed to say they are just *different* requirements.

Even though AS6500 is shorter than AS9100 and has fewer requirements per dollar, you may still feel just a little bit overwhelmed. It's no slouch of a standard. It covers a wide variety of topics. And every requirement is an opportunity to get written up by those devious quality auditors. (All those extra requirements in AS9100 that you thought were such a good bargain provide even more opportunities to fail an audit.)

You may also complain that some of the requirements in AS6500 look a bit similar to AS9100. You would be both right and wrong. As the committee developed AS6500, we tried very hard to not duplicate requirements that were already covered by AS9100. We also ensured there were no conflicts between the standards. Instead, AS6500 provides more detail in some areas that may have only been covered at a very high level in AS9100. AS6500 addresses how some AS9100 requirements must be applied to a manufacturing management program. Examples include process control plans and supplier management. While AS9100 addresses these areas at a high level, AS6500 provides more specific details.

Some overlap is not bad. It emphasizes areas that are vitally important to both a Quality Management System and a Manufacturing Management System. After all, Manufacturing and Quality organizations have similar interests and overlapping responsibilities in some areas. In fact, we should be brothers-in-arms fighting our common enemies in program management and engineering.

As you may have gathered, there are only two things that stand between you and your perfect factory. Program managers and engineers. If only you could bend them to your will, your factory would be humming along like a, uh, smoothly humming metaphorical thing.

Let's start with Program Managers. You may not be aware of this, but Program Managers know MORE about running a factory than you do, even though you may be college-educated with a degree in Manufacturing Engineering and decades of factory experience.

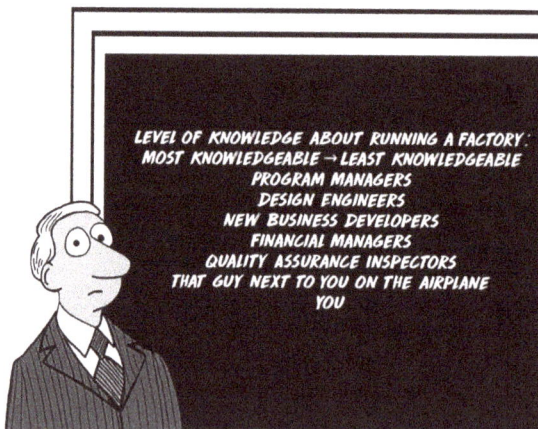

LEVEL OF KNOWLEDGE ABOUT RUNNING A FACTORY:
MOST KNOWLEDGEABLE → LEAST KNOWLEDGEABLE
PROGRAM MANAGERS
DESIGN ENGINEERS
NEW BUSINESS DEVELOPERS
FINANCIAL MANAGERS
QUALITY ASSURANCE INSPECTORS
THAT GUY NEXT TO YOU ON THE AIRPLANE
YOU

© Cartoon Resource

Just because you spent four years in college (oh, who are we kidding—if you're an Industrial Engineer, you were probably on the 5 ½ year track, right? After all, those beers wouldn't drink themselves.) Maybe you even got a master's degree in Manufacturing or Industrial Engineering. And maybe you've spent 30 years on the shop floor, working your way up from a mechanic, to a supervisor, to a planner, to an Industrial Engineer, to a unit manager, to the manager of the whole factory. None of that compares to the vast knowledge possessed by any random Program Manager who majored in Diversity Literature of the Middle Ages.

The superiority of manufacturing knowledge of a PM is easily provable. Just ask them and they will verify it. That's why they are so quick with the advice and so darned authoritative about it.

4

Design Analysis for Manufacturing

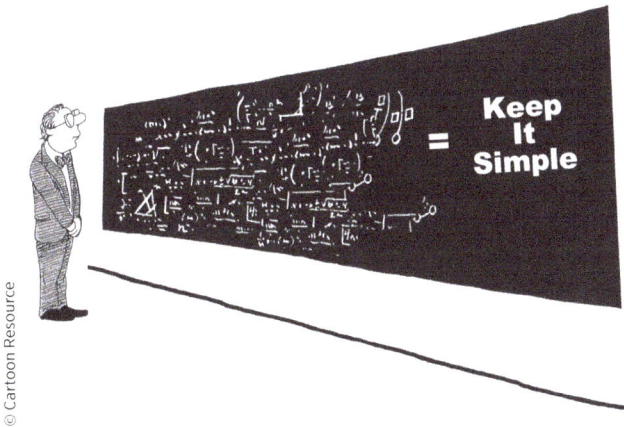

© Cartoon Resource

Program managers aren't the only ones who think they know more about running a factory than a manufacturing engineer or manager. Engineers also think they are experts in manufacturing. But, first, we need to clarify what we mean by engineers:

Enlightened Engineers:

Manufacturing Engineers

Industrial Engineers

Process Engineers

Producibility engineers

Quality Engineers (Quality people are like honorary Manufacturing people)

Welding Engineers (yes, that's a thing)

Engineers from the Dark Side:

Mechanical Engineers
Structural Engineers
Electrical Engineers
Aeronautical Engineers
Hydraulic Engineers
Propulsion engineers
Landing Gear Engineers
Steering Wheel Engineers

The engineer who spends his entire career managing the requirements for ¾" stainless steel screws

Software Engineers get a pass. We, in Manufacturing, don't really build anything they design anyway. In a way, they manufacture their own product; we just upload it to the end item. They can even be helpful in designing and troubleshooting our factory software. Plus, my daughter is a software engineer, so I'm forbidden from making fun of them.

Here's a little more insight into the mind of the Engineers from the Dark Side. I work in an organization that buys stuff (in other words, we don't really design or build anything). Kind of like a gigantic supplier management organization. Many years ago, our Engineering Directorate had to downsize (sound familiar?). Our director decided to eliminate the Manufacturing and Quality Specialists who did not have engineering degrees (which was over half of our entire Manufacturing and Quality workforce). When asked, "Who will do their jobs?" he responded, "Engineers." Because we know that engineers can do anything. Our director actually believed that. "Cover that Manufacturing and Quality stuff? Hey, no problem. We design low observable, super-cruising air superiority aircraft for breakfast; surely, we can handle a little producibility analysis. In fact, we don't even need to do a producibility analysis because, with our advance intelligence and superiority, we just do it automatically. We're so good."

That mindset is the barrier we must overcome, the mountain we have to climb, the river we have to fjord, the ring we have to burn in the fires of Mount Doom.

This is where AS6500 can be your best friend. Boldly stride into the meeting with the Dark Side Engineers, wielding AS6500 like the two-sided lightsaber of Darth Maul. (Sorry for the quick shift from a Lord of the Rings metaphor to a Star Wars metaphor. I'll hold off a while before invoking a Star Trek metaphor. Also, don't take the fact that Darth Maul got chopped in half as a foreshadowing of your ultimate success or failure. Hey, his lightsaber was still cool). You now have an industry standard, a corporate policy, and maybe even a contractual requirement to get your foot in the door of the design review meetings. AS6500 says, "integrate manufacturing into the product design and development process." So now you've got the contractual ammo to get integrated!

AS6500 also says to "engage manufacturing expertise in this process." That's you! I'll let you in on a little secret. The entire SAE G-23 Manufacturing Management Committee was actually thinking of YOU when we wrote this phrase. Yes, YOU. So, don't disappoint us.

Remember, the perfect factory requires the perfect design, and this is your first step to achieving everlasting happiness.

Producibility

What the heck is producibility anyway? If you are Bill Gates and his army of Windows Office designers, you've obviously never even heard of producibility. Just try typing that term into Word. You will most likely get an error and Mr. Gates will helpfully suggest that you meant to type "reducibility." Thanks, Bill, but you're wrong.

So, where do we start? The fundamental question is: Do I even want to undertake a producibility effort in the first place? Let's take a look at the pros and cons.

Cons:

- It's expensive

- It will annoy the dark side engineers (maybe that's a pro)

- It's a lot of work for you. If you don't like your family and don't care to see them often, then maybe this is a pro, too.

- You may need process data that you don't even have

- You may need to get training for your workforce, which is expensive

- You may need to buy some really expensive software tools

Pros:

- The mechanics and technicians in the factory will love you because you're making their work easier. However, they may never realize the horrors you will have saved them from, so they might not love you any more than they already do, which is, hopefully, still a lot.

- The finance managers will love you because you're saving them money. However, they may never realize how much building your product WOULD have cost had you not kept the dark side engineers in check, so they probably also won't love you any more than they do now.

- The program manager will love you because you're helping to ensure they can deliver quality products to the customer on time. However, they will never know what the alternate reality of late deliveries and poor quality would have been like had you not made the changes you did. So, they probably won't love you any more than they do now either, which isn't saying much. But they SHOULD!

Everyone should love you, but they won't! The bottom line is: don't expect to be hailed as a hero because no one will know how much you have saved them. You're only going to experience all the Cons and maybe even make the program and finance managers more unhappy with you because you want more money.

But you will sleep well at night, knowing that you're well on your way to running the perfect factory!

Now that you've committed your time, reputation, and physical well-being to implementing a Producibility Program, where do you go from here?

How you approach producibility depends on where you are in the product life-cycle. If you are in the design phase, you can do more and different things than if you are in production.

Design Phase Producibility

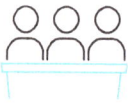

Let's take a look at the concept of producibility. Simply put, this is what Engineers from the Dark Side want to build:

And this is what Manufacturing wants to build:

Shutterstock

You may notice a slight difference in some of the details. Those are the details you must iron out with the designers. They might not respect you at first since they are breathing the rarified air of their lofty position in the company. That just means you have to bring two things to the fight, er, uh, design meetings. First, a 2x4 to hit them upside the head. We are not advocating actual violence; this is just a metaphor. In this case, the symbolic 2x4 would be your company policies that now have robust producibility requirements since they are based on AS6500, which says engineering has to "integrate" you into their secret society.

The second thing to bring is data. Here's where that whole Statistical Process Control (SPC) can really pay off. SPC is one of those tools that everyone talks about, but very few people really implement it—like going to the gym, studying Latin, and eating kale. Everyone boasts about doing those things, but in secret, they just sit on the couch and eat Twinkies. SPC is much more gratifying than kale, so it should be something you want to do.

If you want to make progress towards having the perfect factory, SPC is an important step. Now is the time to make use of all that voluminous data you've been collecting. For example, let's say that the Engineers from the Dark Side want a part that has a length with an overall tolerance of +/- 0.005." Now let's say this is the only tool you have to cut that part:

Shutterstock

Chances are, you're not going to be able to meet those tolerances. But, if you've been collecting data on your Machete MX2000, you can show that you can only hold a tolerance of maybe ± half a foot. That should be enough to convince the Engineers to open those tolerances up just a bit. Or, it might be enough to convince the finance department to open the company wallet up just a bit for a new machine.

Another approach to producibility involves applying some basic producibility principles, such as reducing the number of parts, minimizing the types of fasteners throughout, etc.

A few years ago, we had to get the heat exchanger replaced in our home's furnace. I was amazed when I went down to the basement to check on the progress. It was as if someone had taken every nut, bolt, and screw from the local Home Depot and scattered them across the floor. If I were to collect them all in one pile, it would resemble this photo. And I'm not exaggerating. Imagine my shock when the technician was actually able to reassemble our furnace and get it working again with NO PARTS LEFT OVER and NO NATURAL GAS EXPLOSION. I'm sure that, all along, he was cursing those Engineers from the Dark Side who created such a nightmare.

Shutterstock

On the flip side, we recently got our daughter an electronic piano, with an elegant base for Christmas (some assembly required). I anticipated spending most of Christmas Day assembling her keyboard stand, losing my temper, and cursing like a drunken pirate, even on this most holy day. But much to my surprise, there were only 12 screws and it went together in about 10 minutes. Thank you, Mr. Keyboard Stand Producibility Engineer, wherever you are!

There is another, highly analytical approach to producibility. Mikel J. Harry and J. Ronald Lawson wrote a book called "Six Sigma Producibility Analysis and Process Characterization." I quickly flipped through this book so you wouldn't have to. Here's what I discovered: There's math involved. A lot of math. And the book contains extremely technical terms like, "Dynamic Mean Variation," "Coefficient of the cross-product term of the first and second variable," and "dice." No kidding. This book was written by some very smart guys. Much smarter than me, which isn't necessarily a high bar. But, to implement these tools, you have to be smart and know math, especially statistics.

Here's a bonus tip for which you don't have to pay any extra money: Never take a class in Statistics from a guy who wrote his own textbook. It can only end badly. Chances are (see my fluent use of statistics?) either you, the professor, or his beloved book will have serious flaws which will lead to a grade lower (maybe much lower) than what you were hoping for.

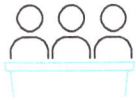

But don't let my lack of statistical expertise dissuade you from following Mr. Harry's and Mr. Lawson's book. Just carrying it around with you will impress everyone. To the Engineers from the Dark Side, it will make you look like you're one of them. You may even be able to infiltrate their super-secret Engineers of the Dark Side Coffee Club. And to Program Managers, you will appear to be a bonafide guru and they will fear talking to you. The book is truly insightful and groundbreaking, and you should really buy it, even if you don't use it. One aspect of the perfect factory is to have all the right books on the shelf. But in all fairness, any material by Boothroyd and Dewhurst on Design for Manufacturing and Assembly has prettier pictures.

Mandatory legal disclaimer: The author of this book receives zero financial remuneration from promoting "Six Sigma Producibility Analysis and Process Characterization" and Boothroyd and Dewhurst's "Design for Manufacturing and Assembly," although he really should because he really likes both of those books and really thinks you should buy them.

© Cartoon Resource

Production Phase Producibility

If your product is in production, it's too late for producibility. Well, maybe not. You obviously have fewer opportunities to change the design, but all is not lost. All you need is a bucket of money. A big bucket of money. As the famous philosopher Steve Martin said when asked how to become a millionaire, "First, get a million dollars."

If your program manager is reluctant to shovel piles of money your way, you may consider asking your customer, assuming your customer is a company or government organization that has deeper pockets than you. As unlikely to succeed as this sounds, it's actually been done many times in the past. Customers may be willing to fork over (i.e., "invest") if there is an advantageous sharing arrangement for the savings. Your company may have to promise them a healthy return on their investment, your first-born child, and season tickets to the New England Patriots games, which may soon be a dated joke.

Now that you have the BoM (Bucket of Money, not to be confused with Bill of Material), what to do with it? Here's where all your dreams and fantasies come to life. Not the ones where you are alone on a desert island, except for your personal butler and movie star companion. The ones where you wish you could redesign that One Darn Feature (ODF) that causes so many headaches in the factory. Get rid of some parts? Open up some tolerances? Get that shiny new machine with lasers? Those are some of the Producibility Improvement Projects (or PIPS, which hopefully hasn't already been copyrighted by some big company with lawyers) that you can now finally implement. All you have to do is hope and pray that the savings you predicted come to fruition, because your customer will be expecting them through eternity.

Key Characteristics

Have you ever thought back to the favorite meeting you've ever attended? Of course not. No sane person does. In fact, no one could even possibly HAVE a favorite meeting. As Dilbert has said, meetings are full of soul-crushing boredom and futility. Except for one, small, shining exception. And it relates to a requirement of AS6500.

Many years ago, I worked on a program that was required to identify Key Characteristics (KCs). To fully understand Key Characteristics, you should purchase the fine, outstanding publication from SAE, AS9103, "Key Characteristics and Variation Reduction." Even though I receive no royalties from that standard either, I still highly recommend it.

Anyway, the best meeting I ever attended came about as a result of the need to identify KCs. Whether or not a feature is a KC can be driven by numerous factors. One of those factors is how part mates with another part. In the meeting in question, we had both design engineers AND manufacturing engineers from multiple Integrated Product Teams (whose parts all had to be assembled together) IN THE SAME ROOM! I'm not even talking by telecon or Video Telecon. They were actually close enough to reach across the conference table to strangle each other if needed. Strangely, they all got along well, and they talked about how the various part features would mate with each other, which tolerances were the most critical, and how well they could be controlled during fabrication. It was almost unnatural watching them interact.

And what brought together these groups that were normally as friendly to each other as the Montagues and the Capulets? Key Characteristics. Yes, KCs can bring together Montagues and Capulets, Catholics and Protestants, Republicans, and Democrats.

The result of all those meetings about Key Characteristics was that the very first set of parts "fit like a glove" (this was an actual quote from one of the shop floor supervisors.) See? This stuff actually works.

At this point, those of you in the electronics industry have nearly fallen asleep or have skipped this section entirely. You've been thinking, "Oh sure, this whole key characteristics thing is fine for metal, plastic, or composite parts. We don't cut and drill; we pick, place, and solder. For you mechanical engineers, it's simple to slap a KC on a physical part dimension."

Say, for example, a machined aluminum part. A mechanical engineer can identify the thickness of the part, the length, or even the surface finish as a Key Characteristic (KC). But, unlike those metal-benders, electronics companies make circuit cards that don't seem to lend themselves to KCs, so they must not apply, right? Au Contraire. You can't get off the hook so easily.

KCs can be applied to electronics in two ways. The first is to its physical characteristics. No, not the dimensions of the circuit card, but rather the characteristics of the solder joint (such as the solder thickness, land height, etc.) which can be measured and tracked through typical inspection methods. The second approach is to identify electrical characteristics (responses to inputs, voltages, currents, response times, etc.) as KCs, which can be measured through functional testing. None of this is as easy as pulling out your trusty micrometer to measure the thickness of a part, but you'll feel good about yourself in the end.

Since Key Characteristics are an important part of your perfect factory, what does AS6500 have to say about them? Because AS6500 is an AEROSPACE standard, you must expect it to include some requirements on, well, AEROSPACE. If you are not involved in building airplanes, helicopters, or hot air balloons, or you don't care about the safety of the flying public or our brave men and women in the cockpits, you can ignore this next section. Go ahead. Skip down a few paragraphs and wait. We'll catch up.

The requirement for KCs shows up on the design analysis section of AS6500. Specifically, the standard requires key or critical characteristics to be identified "for Critical Safety Items and Critical Application Items to help control the quality of the CSIs and CAIs."

Just to make it easy on you and refresh your memory on some of these terms, here's a little game. Match the definition to the correct term:

Term	Definition
Key Characteristic	The features of a material or part whose variation has a significant influence on product fit, performance, service life, or manufacturability
Critical Characteristic	A characteristic that is likely, if defective, to create or increase a hazard to human safety, or to result in failure of a system to perform a required function
Critical Safety Item	A part or assembly whose failure or malfunction could cause a catastrophic or critical failure resulting in loss of life, permanent disability or major injury, loss of a system, or significant equipment damage
Critical Application Item	A part or assembly essential to system performance or operation, or the preservation of life or safety of operating personnel
Manufacturing Management Program	No fair, go check AS6500 as I told you in the last chapter

This was a trick question. The correct definition is directly across from each term. We didn't want you to have to think too hard, at least not yet.

This requirement for KCs wasn't just from one of the young, idealistic members of the committee, nor was it from one of the old grouchy codgers. It's actually based on Federal Law. Sort of. That's right. Public Law 108-136, Sec 802, says that Critical Characteristics must be identified for CSIs on Department of Defense programs. Otherwise, you might be headed to jail without collecting $200. Well, probably not. But it's still a darned good idea.

Here are a few little plot twists. If you read the law carefully, the requirement is to identify CRITICAL characteristics for CSIs. But AS6500 says you can identify key or critical characteristics. We think either of those, which satisfy the intent of the law. At least, that's what you can tell the Federal Marshalls when they come to arrest you.

The second plot twist is that AS6500 says that, "The same controls required by this standard for KCs shall be applied to critical characteristics." We mainly said that so everywhere in the standard we didn't have to keep typing "key and/or critical characteristics." Well, not really. But some organizations use critical characteristics to a much larger extent than just for CSIs, so, since they went through the trouble of identifying them, it's up to you and your perfect factory to control those critical characteristics to make them as perfect as possible.

To help you in better identifying key characteristics, here are some frequently asked questions:

Q: How many lawyers does it take to identify a key characteristic?

A: Judging by how some companies do it, apparently it takes ALL of them. On one extreme, some companies say they have no KCs because they've all been designed away, which is like saying there are no spiders in my basement; they all moved outside. As much as I would like to believe this (and you have NO IDEA how much I would like to believe this – my daughters love to buy realistic plastic spiders and place them around the house just to watch me scream in terror like a little girl), I have a really hard time believing it's true.

On the other extreme, I've heard tales of terror where a company has mandated "X" number of KCs be identified by their suppliers, where "X" is a real, non-zero number greater than, oh, say, one hundred.

In reality, we don't need more lawyers (except for any wonderful lawyers who are reading this book. I'm sure YOU are a FINE lawyer and a credit to your profession) to interpret contractual requirements for KCs. We just need design and manufacturing engineers to talk to each other and determine what features are most affected by variation from nominal (don't you like how that definition just rolls off the tongue?)

continues

continued

> **Q:** How many KCs should my product have?

> **A:** 42.
>
> After all, that's the answer to life, the universe, and everything, according to Douglas Adams.

> **Q:** If a process is capable, does the KC go away?

> **A:** Have you ever seen one of the Dilbert cartoons where Dogbert whacks an employee upside the head with a rolled-up newspaper? Well, if this is your question, lean over here so I can reach you…

The definition of a KC has nothing to do with the capability of the process that creates it. Let me say that again. The definition of a KC has nothing to do with the capability of the process that creates it. How about a few more times?

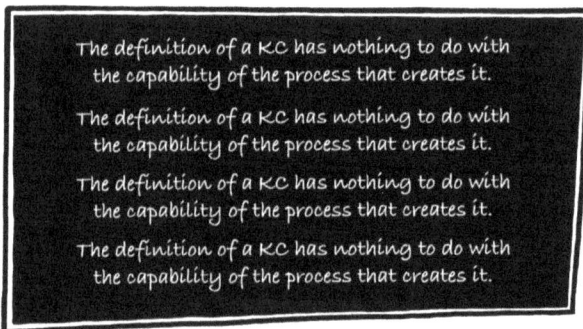

This might bear repeating a few more times.

The definition of a KC has nothing to do with the capability of the process that creates it.

The definition of a KC has nothing to do with the capability of the process that creates it.

The definition of a KC has nothing to do with the capability of the process that creates it.

The definition of a KC has nothing to do with the capability of the process that creates it.

The definition of a KC has everything to do with the design of the feature and its impact on the performance of the product. If I could put this on a banner and fly it over football games, I would. Can you tell that this is a frequent area of frustration?

Q: There are so many different definitions of Key Characteristics in multiple documents. Which one is correct?

A: "Take a look inside your heart. There's an answer in your heart." That's the advice from the second greatest rock band to come out of Canada, Triumph, in their song "Fight the Good Fight." Of course, they do deserve some abuse for rhyming "heart" and "heart." But the intent is good. Your heart says to not get hung up on small differences in definitions. Go on. Take a look. That's what it's saying. The important thing is to not lose sight of the whole purpose of KCs, which is to apply the Pareto principle and focus process control efforts on the most critical features.

Q: Now that you've brought it up, what's the greatest rock band to come out of Canada?

A: Do you even need to ask? Rush. (RIP Neil Peart.)

There are a few other, more obscure analysis tools that can also lead you to a perfectly producible design. The problem is, I'm not sure anyone has ever really used them. Raise your hand if you've ever actually used the Taguchi Loss Function to calculate a tolerance or if you've actually constructed a "house of quality" using Quality Function Deployment? Anyone? Anyone? But I bet you studied them in some Quality class.

How about Design of Experiments (DOEs)? OK, I see a few hands raised on that one. Good job. Keep up the good work. Sadly, the only time I ever used DOE was in the DOE class. We experimented on how to get the best results when popping popcorn on the stove, using oil (not the dry, boring, air-popped method.) If you want to get your money's worth on a per-kernel-popped basis, we found that it was really worth it to pay for the name brand stuff. (You're welcome, Mr. Redenbacher!)

It's sad that we learn all these great and wonderful techniques and then so rarely get to implement them. It's like when you tell your kids to not touch the stove when it's hot, don't lick the gum on the underside of a restaurant table, or don't buy a used Chevy Vega. You have so much wisdom, but no one pays attention. Maybe this is your opportunity to try something new. So, dust off those old Quality seminar notebooks and ask some hotshot kid to program MATLAB for you to calculate a Taguchi Loss Function!

Process Failure Modes Effects Analyses (PFMEA)

You've all heard of Design Failure Modes Effects Analysis (DFMEA), right? It's the process that design engineers go through to determine all the different ways a product could break or malfunction, the resulting effects, and the possible design changes to keep the really bad things from happening. Everybody loves Design FMEAs. In fact, you don't even have to say "Design FMEAs." If you just say "FMEAs" everyone assumes you're talking about design FMEAs. So, let's be honest, Process FMEAs are the ugly stepchildren of the Design FMEAs. Design FMEAs are the "perfect older sibling." Why can't Process FMEAs be more like them? Design FMEAs are like Batman; Process FMEAs are like the garishly dressed, slightly odd Robin, the wisecracking sidekick that no one takes seriously and who ruined a perfectly good Dark Knight detective image of Batman. Not to mention ruining a few Batman movies. Process FMEAs are like Robin screaming, "Hey, I'm a super-hero, too!"

Who really does PFMEAs? I've been told that the automotive industry does them as a way of life, but aerospace? Raise your hand if you are in the aerospace industry and you routinely do Process FMEAs. Anyone? Anyone? Buehler?

But from now on, YOU will be different. YOU will do Process FMEAs because they are another key ingredient to running the perfect factory.

So, what are they? Process FMEAs are a structured approach to analyzing what could possibly go wrong with a manufacturing process, the impacts of those errors, and what could be done to prevent them. If you want to learn the details of how to perform Process FMEAs, buy SAE International's J1739 standard, "Potential Failure Mode and Effects Analysis in Design (Design FMEA), Potential Failure Mode and Effects Analysis in Manufacturing and Assembly Processes (Process FMEA)." Yes, that's one heck of a mouthful. Since I don't get any money if you buy this standard, you know my endorsement is given with heartfelt sincerity.

Despite their second-class citizen status, Process FMEAs can be extremely powerful. Here is a real-life, no kidding, no exaggeration, true story: A certain prime contractor purchased an electronic component from a supplier that had four female connectors coming out of it. When it was delivered to them, they assembled it by attaching the male connectors to the female connectors. The problem was the connectors had to be connected to their specific mate, but they were identically shaped. Although the part numbers were printed on the wires and listed in the work instructions as to which connectors matched up, they were often miscon-nected. The solution? Color code the connectors! Great! How hard could it be to match blue with blue, green with green, etc.? It's like Grrranimals as a kid. A child could do it.

Well, apparently not. The company found they were still being misconnected. After some investigation, they realized that one of their technicians was color blind! Aha! Problem identified! Well, once again, apparently not. It turned out the color-blind employee was the only one to NOT make any mistakes! He knew his limitations, so he was especially careful to make sure they were correctly attached by closely paying attention to the part numbers.

The company realized that had they performed a process FMEA, they would have predicted this problem. Their ultimate solution was to redesign the connectors so they would only match their correct counterpart so they could NOT be connected incorrectly. If they had done a PFMEA earlier, they would have saved a great deal of time and money. The power of Process FMEAs!

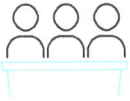

But if you still really aren't sold on PFMEAs, or if you are an Engineer from the Dark Side who want them to fail, then here are some ways that you can ensure that your Process FMEAs are useless:

1. Wait until it's too late to do them. Yes, it's never really too late, but the more you put off doing them, the more you can enjoy the stress of dealing with late, non-conforming parts that are killing your budget.

2. Pencil whip them. Just jump to the easy, obvious failure modes of the process and don't try to be creative and come up with those obscure, one-in-a-million failures that will never happen, because nothing unlikely ever goes wrong.

3. Settle on weak recommendations, like just adding more inspections. Those will catch everything.

4. Don't bother really implementing the preventive actions. They're too hard and may cost money. Just keep relying on those inspections.

5. When changes to the product or process occur, don't bother updating the PFMEA. Those changes probably won't be a big deal, right?

5

Manufacturing Risk Identification

"Well, now we know what not to do."

Manufacturing Readiness Level (MRL) Assessments

As the manager of the perfect factory, you are all over MRLs. Not only do you know your MRL target, but you've also surpassed your target!

For those of you who don't know what MRLs are, go ahead and climb out from under that rock right now. MRLs are only the greatest thing to happen in the manufacturing world since Henry Ford invented the assembly line. If we give them enough time, MRLs will eventually solve world hunger.

If you're not familiar with MRLs, we'll go through a little primer. If you are familiar with them, you can skip this next section, but, sorry to say, you won't get a rebate on the purchase price of this book.

**SKIP THIS PART IF YOU KNOW
ALL ABOUT MRLs!
WE'LL CATCH UP WITH
YOU LATER! BYE!**

Here's what the Department of Defense's MRL Deskbook has to say about MRLs:

Assessments of manufacturing readiness utilizing the Manufacturing Readiness Level (MRL) criteria have been designed to manage manufacturing risk in acquisition while increasing the ability of the technology development projects to transition new technology to weapon system applications. MRL criteria create a measurement scale and vocabulary for assessing and discussing manufacturing maturity and risk. Using the MRL criteria, an assessment of manufacturing readiness is a structured evaluation of a technology, component, manufacturing process, weapon system, or subsystem. It is performed to:

- *Define the current level of manufacturing maturity*

- *Identify maturity shortfalls and associated costs and risks*

- *Provide the basis for manufacturing maturation and risk management*

The first thing you will notice from this description from the MRL Deskbook is the lack of humor. In fact, the entire MRL Deskbook has zero jokes. That makes it a little bit hard to read. It was written by a great bunch of people who are very funny in real life, but sadly, official DoD publications are no places for jokes. (Feel free to insert your own joke here about DoD publications.) As a side note, wouldn't government and company policies be much more fun with a little humor thrown in?

Stodgy policy title	Better policy title
"10,000 lb Drill Press - Emergency Medical Procedures"	"So you lost a finger in a machine. Now what?"
"Supplier Selection Process"	"Graft, Nepotism, and Bribery – How to Best Choose a Supplier that Works for YOU"
"Personnel Hiring Process"	"Graft, Nepotism, and Bribery – How to Best Choose an Employee that Works for YOU"
"Producibility Considerations in the Design Process"	"How to get those D*** Design Engineers to Shut up and Listen"

Well, that was a bit of a departure from a discussion on MRLs. And the people that are skipping this section are missing out on comedy gold. But now back to the regularly scheduled, boring discourse on MRLs.

MRL determinations are made through the evaluation of nine topic areas, called threads. The MRL Deskbook dryly explains each thread:

- *Technology and the Industrial Base: Requires an analysis of the capability of the national technology and industrial base to support the design, development, production, operation, uninterrupted maintenance support of the system, and eventual disposal (environmental impacts).*

- *Design: Requires an understanding of the producibility, maturity, and stability of the evolving system design, identification, and control of Key Characteristics, and any related impact on manufacturing readiness.*

- *Cost and Funding: Requires an analysis of the adequacy of funding to achieve target manufacturing maturity levels. Examines the risks associated with reaching manufacturing cost targets.*

- *Materials: Requires an analysis of the risks associated with materials (including basic/raw materials, components, semi-finished parts, and subassemblies).*

- *Process Capability and Control: Requires an analysis of the risks that the manufacturing processes can reflect the design intent (repeatability and affordability) of key characteristics.*

- *Quality: Requires an analysis of the risks and management efforts to control quality, and foster continuous improvement.*

- *Manufacturing Workforce (Engineering and Production): Requires an assessment of the required skills, availability, and required number of personnel to support the manufacturing effort.*

- *Facilities: Requires an analysis of the capabilities and capacity of key manufacturing facilities (prime, subcontractor, supplier, vendor, and maintenance/repair).*

- *Manufacturing Management: Requires an analysis of the orchestration of all elements needed to translate the design into an integrated and fielded system (meeting Program goals for affordability and availability). Many of the MRL threads have been decomposed into sub-thread*

One last boring explanation: MRL Assessments are conducted throughout the program life cycle. The threads are arranged in a matrix with objective criteria provided for each thread and level to reflect the growing expectation of maturity as the program progresses through its life cycle. In the early phases of product development, manufacturing feasibility is the only expectation. As a program progresses through development, the MRL criteria become more stringent and production representative manufacturing processes are anticipated.

If this well-told explanation is not clear enough, you can go to the MRL website, dodmrl.com, for everything you ever wanted to know about MRLs.

FOR THOSE OF YOU WHO SKIPPED AHEAD, YOU CAN REJOIN US NOW.

One of the most important things to know about MRLs is most program managers don't like them and will resist you with every fiber of their being. In fact, we can actually demonstrate the level of resistance you will receive when you propose performing an MRL assessment to a program manager. Our crack investigative team at SAE International and the G-23 Manufacturing Management Committee was able to secretly install hidden microphones in the office of one typical program manager. We recorded the actual conversation when he was asked by the Manufacturing Engineer about doing an MRL assessment at one of their supplier's facilities.

The following transcript has not been changed or edited. The names have been omitted to protect both the guilty and the heroic.

Manufacturing Engineer: Uh, excuse me, sir?

Program Manager: (Loud, thundering voice with loads of echo and reverb) Who dares approach the great and powerful Oz?

SIDE NOTE: Apparently, this program manager's name was Fred Ozmodius.

Manufacturing Engineer: It's me, _____ (name withheld by request.)

Program Manager: And who might you be?

Manufacturing Engineer: I, uh, work in the Manufacturing Engineering department and we're bringing on a new supplier. So, we think we should conduct an MRL Assessment on them.

Program Manager: What? Why would you want to do that?

Manufacturing Engineer: To see if they're ready to go into production.

Program Manager: Don't be foolish. Of course, they are ready. Their CEO told me so himself as we were sharing steak and lobster at his summer home in the Bahamas.

Manufacturing Engineer: Well, sir, I don't mean to question him, but that might not be sufficient. We should probably go out ourselves to verify that.

Program Manager: And just how much is this assessment going to cost? You know our budget is tight.

Manufacturing Engineer: I don't know exactly. It will certainly be a few thousand dollars.

Program Manager: What??

Manufacturing Manager: But think of it this way. It's a small investment to know what risks are out there with this supplier. We don't want to be surprised when they can't meet their delivery commitments.

Program Manager: As an all-knowing, all-seeing program manager, I happen to know a little bit about this MRL process myself. What if you go out there and find that they are not at MRL 8, which is where they have to be for production. Are you going to tell me they can't do the job and not give them the contract? Where would we be then? Huh?

Manufacturing Manager: It doesn't work that way. This is just a risk assessment. It's not a pass/fail test. If they're not where they're supposed to be, we'll figure out how much risk there is and get them on a risk reduction plan. But at least we'll know and won't be surprised.

Program Manager: Hmmm. Very well. I'm not happy about this at all, but I reluctantly and begrudgingly give my approval.

Manufacturing Manager: Thank you, oh mighty Oz. By the way, would you like to go along with the review?

Program Manager: Say what?

Manufacturing Manager: You should come along. I think you might learn a few things.

Program Manager: Are they located near a golf course?

Manufacturing Manager: I'm sure we could find you one nearby.

Program Manager: Very well, then, I shall accompany you.

And that's exactly how it went. Fortunately, our tape recorders were still rolling when the program manager returned from the trip:

Manufacturing Manager: Hey, Frank, I mean, great and powerful Oz. What did you think of the MRL assessment?

Program Manager: Oh, you can drop the "great and powerful Oz" stuff. I had a great time! Man, that MRL review was AWESOME! I learned so much! I had no idea how they made their products! Why didn't you tell me about these MRL reviews before? I'm going to mandate that we do MRL assessments on EVERY supplier!

Manufacturing Manager: I don't think we need to do that. It would be expensive to do it for everyone.

Program Manager: Nonsense! This stuff is like gold! No, platinum! No, vibranium! Get me the CEOs of all our suppliers on the phone. I'm going to tell them we expect them to do a bang-up job on these reviews and I'm going to personally attend each and every review.

Ok, so I'll admit that I took some creative license with that first discussion, but I've had program managers make those arguments (and more) to try to avoid doing MRLs. The follow-up discussion, however, was not actually that far from the truth, except for the vibranium reference. Once program managers get out of their cushy offices and go out to suppliers on MRL assessments, I've seen them do a complete 180. They suddenly love MRLs! After all, what's not to love? At this point in the history of manufacturing, I think it's safe to say that everyone who is anyone is doing MRLs.

This is the part of the book where I tell you about the funniest stories that have happened at MRL reviews. Strap yourselves in and prepare to laugh yourself silly at the madcap misadventures that often happen during an assessment. Are you ready? Here goes…

Sadly, there are no funny MRL stories. As comedians like to say, there's no humor down that road. It's a comedic dead end. MRL reviews are usually very professional (i.e., boring). Not that it's a dull time getting to see the coolest factories that are making the most modern, cutting edge technologies; it's just that it's not a laugh-a-minute joke-fest that would lend a lot of humorous stories to this book. In all my MRL reviews, I've never seen drunken attendees dancing on the conference table.

If, by chance, you DO have some humorous stories, please let me know and I'll include them in "Running the Perfect Factory, Part II, Management Strikes Back."

In all seriousness, it is a joy and honor to visit many of the companies that have hosted us for MRL reviews. American industry is producing items of incredible complexity and it is exciting to see what many of you Manufacturing professionals have accomplished. But because many of the products are so advanced, and everyone understands that there are challenges to producing these complex, tight-tolerance products, we need MRLs to understand those challenges. It's not simple stuff. MRLs help us to collectively (customer, primes, and suppliers) understand where the risks are and what manufacturing development and maturation activities still need to be accomplished.

The hardest part of the entire MRL process is to determine where to actually perform MRL assessments. In other words, what suppliers, components, or processes should you review? The MRL Deskbook has a very helpful list of questions you can use to screen each candidate to determine if you should go there. The Deskbook calls it determining the assessment "Taxonomy," which is an overly officious-sounding word that means, "Where to do MRL assessments."

You may notice that this list roughly parallels the MRL threads. This probably isn't a coincidence.

Here is the suggested list of questions from the deskbook:

☑ Materials: Are there materials that have not been demonstrated in similar products or manufacturing processes?

☑ Cost: Is this item a driver that significantly impacts lifecycle cost (development, unit, or operations and support costs)? Is technology new with high-cost uncertainty?

☑ Design: Is the item design novel or does it contain nonstandard dimensions or tolerances or arrangements?

☑ Manufacturing Process: Will the item require the use of manufacturing technology, processes, inspection, or capabilities that are unproven in the current environment?

☑ Quality: Does the item have historical/anticipated yield or quality issues?

☑ Schedule: Does this item have lead time issues or does it significantly impact the schedule?

☑ Facilities: Does this item require a new manufacturing facility or scale-up of existing facilities (i.e., new capability or capacity)?

☑ Supply Chain Management: Does the item have anticipated or historical sub-tier supplier problems (e.g., cost, quality, delivery)?

☑ Industrial Base: Does the item have an industrial base footprint with critical shortfalls or is this a critical item manufactured by a sole or foreign source?

So, as a service to you, faithful reader, I have compiled a few additional questions you should consider in determining if you should go to a supplier to perform an assessment:

☑ How's the weather in the destination city?

☑ What major golf courses are available there?

☑ What food is the city noted for?

☑ Is the supplier located in Las Vegas? (An automatic trigger for an on-site review.)

☑ How much will I make in per diem? (Los Angeles can be profitable; Wichita, Kansas, not so much.)

☑ Will the review take place while my in-laws are visiting from out-of-town?

If you answer "Yes" to any one of the questions, that doesn't mean that your program is doomed, and you had better be on the next flight to go see this supplier. But the more "Yes's" you answer, the more you should consider performing an MRL assessment.

The problem is, I find this list to be inadequate. It seems to miss a few areas of consideration.

Feel free to weight these questions to meet your desires. For me, the question of "food" is very important. I'll gladly sign up for a trip to Fort Worth, Texas, just to get some great BBQ. Some of you may prefer New England for Lobster, the southwest for Mexican, Italy for Italian, or Great Britain for, well, uhh, never mind.

Your peers will not have this list of additional criteria and may make poor decisions about where to go. You, on the other hand, armed with this insightful list, will be jetting off to the absolute best locations, while your colleagues will be suffering in Minot, North Dakota, in February. (This really happened to me. I should not have foolishly agreed to travel to the god-forsaken, wind-swept tundra of North Dakota two days after a major blizzard.)

Once you go onsite, you'll need to have a game plan that you've coordinated with all the participants. The best way to do this is to develop an agenda that everyone can agree to. As our never-ending dedication to help you, fearless manufacturing manager, here is a sample agenda:

SAMPLE MRL REVIEW AGENDA	
9:00	Sign in
9:15 – 9:45	Full, catered breakfast
9:45 – 10:00	Introductions
10:00 – 10:30	Break
10:30 – 11:00	Review self-assessment
11:00 – 1:00	Full, catered lunch
1:00 – 2:00	Guided plant tour, preferably with golf cart transportation provided
2:00 – 2:15	Assessment team private caucus to summarize findings, with emphasis on the quality of food and factory tour
2:15 – 2:30	Outbrief supplier, dump action items on them, and depart for golf course

© SAE International

CHAPTER 6

Interlude

SHERLOCK HOLMES
and the
Adventure of the
Failing Factory

© Cartoon Resource

Interlude: A word which here means a pause in the normal flow of a book that should not be skipped because its message is integral to the message of the entire book and it is most definitely not an opportunity for the writer to be self-indulgent in something he has always wanted to write.

Sherlock Holmes and the Adventure of the Failing Factory

My friend Sherlock Holmes has helped to capture many unique and devious criminals, but none so sly and diabolical as the villain he discovered in his most recent adventure. Even the evil Moriarty made himself more plainly known as the force behind London's most famous crime sprees. The average hooligan may relieve a few individuals of their purse or a bank of its well-insured assets, but this vandal nearly robbed over 300 hardworking, salt-of-the-earth families of their livelihood.

It began on a cold, foggy Monday morning at 10 am as Mrs. Hudson had just brought us our tea and mid-morning biscuits. Holmes was staring out the window as he often does to take in all that is happening in the city. He prided himself on knowing the intricacies and the goings-on in greater London.

"Watson," he said. "We are about to be visited by a most desperate man in need of our services."

I said nothing, with the full knowledge that he was correct, and merely waited on Mrs. Hudson to announce our desperate visitor. Sure enough, moments later, she arrived at our door with a plain-looking man in his 50s, dressed in an oxford shirt, unbuttoned at the top, suit jacket, and overcoat.

Mrs. Hudson introduced him as Mr. Thaddeus Whitmore. As she turned to leave, we each made our introductions.

Once we were seated, Holmes bluntly stated, "I see that your machining company is failing, Mr. Whitmore and the banks have refused any additional loans."

Our guest seemed quite taken aback, sputtering, and stumbling over his words. "But, Mr. Holmes, I have been so careful to keep this out of the papers and trade journals. How on earth did you hear of it?"

"I haven't," Homes replied. "It's quite obvious."

Once again, our guest sputtered and looked around the room and then looked himself up and down for what he thought must have been a neon sign with the news beaming from his person. I merely sat back and chuckled to myself.

Seeing the man's quizzical look, Homes took pity on him and explained. "Your clothes are from the finest tailor in town, indicating a man of senior authority and means. But I notice the small metal filings embedded in the bottom of your shoes, indicating you spend time on the factory floor of a metal processing facility."

"That's right. Mr. Holmes. I am the owner and manager of South London Metalworks. I like to occasionally get out of my office and mingle with my workers to see how things are going. But how could you know of our finances?"

"As my friend and colleague Dr. Watson here like to imagine that I say, but which I do not, it is elementary."

"You do say that, Holmes," I interjected.

"I do not, Watson."

"Oh, you most certainly do. And quite frequently."

Homes harrumphed and returned to Mr. Whitmore's question. "Nevertheless, it is quite an el…, uh, obvious." Holmes gave me a sly look. "You arrived here at 10 am on a Monday morning with obvious urgency. You have no tie on, but your open shirt collar reveals a redness of your neck indicating that you did have your shirt buttoned to your neck, presumably to accommodate a tie, but have removed it very shortly before coming here. As the banks open at 9 am, I surmise that, after suffering through the weekend with your knowledge of financial distress, you arrived immediately upon their opening with a suit, jacket, and tie to make the most positive impression of all. But since you are nowhere without your tie, I can see that your pleadings with them have failed and you removed your tie in frustration, no longer having any need of it."

"My word, Mr. Holmes, you are surely a wizard!"

"On the contrary, sir. I rely on no supernatural sources for my deductions. Now, pray tell me about your situation."

"Oh, Mr. Holmes, I am ruined. And not just me, but all of the wonderful people that work for me. I can't bear the thought of what this will do to them and their families. But let me back up.

"As I said, I am the owner of South London Metalworks. My grandfather started the company during the war and built it into quite a successful business. I began working there as a youth and worked through all of the departments until my father retired and handed me the reigns, some 10 years ago. We have, of course, had our challenges through the ups and downs of economies, but we have generally been quite profitable. At least until about two years ago."

"What happened then?" I asked.

"That's just the thing, Mr. Watson. Nothing. Nothing changed. It took a few months to realize it, but we were beginning to lose money. It has only gotten worse. Now I fear I cannot save the business."

"Surely you must have some ideas of wrongdoing, Mr. Whitmore, or you would not be here talking to a consulting detective," Holmes said.

Whitmore paused and sighed. "Mr. Holmes, I can hardly put this into words, but I suspect that one of my senior vice presidents is…is…is embezzling from the company."

"With 300 employees, why have you narrowed it down to only three?" Holmes asked.

"Because those three are the only employees with full access and authority in our ERP system." Seeing my confused look, he explained, "Our Enterprise Resource Planning system, Dr. Watson. That's the computer system that, in effect, runs our company. It determines when we order raw materials, when it gets scheduled for production, how many people we need, and keeps track of all the financial transactions."

Holmes said, "So tell me about these three individuals."

Whitmore replied, "I suppose you could rightly call them suspects, Mr. Holmes, but I can't bear to think of them that way. The first is Frank Jergens, my VP for

Production Operations. He has been with the company for almost 30 years. He's a crusty old bird, but he knows his stuff and I absolutely trust him to run the day-to-day operations of the factory.

"Harold Dexter is my VP for Engineering. He's only been with us for four years, but he's straight as an arrow, Mr. Holmes. Very knowledgeable. Very dedicated. I can't imagine him or Frank stealing from the company."

"What about the third VP, Mr. Whitmore?" I asked.

"The third VP is actually my daughter, Carrie. Carrie Sutherland. She runs the Finance department."

Holmes asked, "And how are your family relationships with her?"

"Wonderful, Mr. Holmes! I couldn't ask for a better, more capable, competent, and loving daughter. So, you see, gentlemen, of the three people who are capable, I don't believe any of them would do such a thing."

"We shall see, Mr. Whitmore. The human heart is, at its core, totally depraved, but yet we have an amazing capability to shield that ugly side from others," Holmes said.

Whitmore looked crestfallen. "I understand, sir. I shall accept whatever you find."

Holmes rose. "Mr. Whitmore, I should like to visit your fine company and talk to these three individuals. Feel free to be open with them about the reason for my visit. Shall we say first thing tomorrow morning? Good. Dr. Watson and I shall see you then."

South London Metalworks was located in an industrial park, surrounded by other similar, non-descript looking buildings. Holmes and I entered and introduced ourselves to the receptionist who paged Mr. Whitmore. The man arrived shortly, dressed much more casually and comfortably in a dark blue golf shirt with a set of earplugs dangling around his neck and safety glasses resting atop his head.

"Thank you for coming, gentlemen. Might I give you a tour before we start?"

"Perhaps later, Mr. Whitmore. First, we should proceed with meeting your key staff members," Holmes said.

"Very well. Right this way."

He led us along a narrow hallway that ran the length of the front of the building. We passed by a set of double doors through which we could glimpse the factory.

Holmes leaned over to me and said, "I suppose, Watson, that the factory is typically a foreign landscape to most medical men, but your brief stint at Bryce Foundry prior to medical school has prepared you for this."

"How did you know, Holmes? It was so brief a job that I don't believe I ever recounted it to you?"

"Simple, Watson. I saw you slip those old safety glasses into your pocket before we left our flat. They have the name of the foundry on the side. And since I don't know of any other gaps in your history of when you would have time to work there, it is only logical that you were there during the summer before medical school to earn money." Of course, he was right.

We arrived at a suite of offices that were furnished, not extravagantly, but nicer than those we had been walking past.

Mr. Whitmore led us into the first office with the name "Frank Jurgens" posted on the door. Jurgens was a portly man with a scruffy beard, unkempt hair, dressed in a polo shirt and jeans. He sported ear and eye protection matching Mr. Whitmore's.

He only half stood up to reach across his desk with his big, beefy hand to perfunctorily shake ours. He plopped back down without offering us seats.

"Whitmore here told me why you've come. You're wasting your time and mine. I've got nothing to do with the poor finances of this place. In fact, I bust my butt to get our orders delivered outta here on time. No offense to Mr. Whitmore and his daughter, but I believe it's the bean counters that mucked things up.

"In fact, it's absolutely foolish to hire a detective. What we need is a new accountant. And we certainly don't need any of your parlor tricks, Mr. Sherlock Holmes. Now if you will excuse me, I have a factory to run."

Holmes calmly said, "Of course, Mr. Jurgens, I completely understand. We shall trouble you no further."

Whitmore had been waiting in the hallway during Jurgens' small diatribe. As we left the office, Whitmore tried to make apologies for Jurgens' behavior. I was rather shocked at Holmes' deferential attitude towards the portly production manager and his lack of questions for him. Even though he had been a trusted employee for many years, he seemed overly protective, as if he may have something to hide.

We rounded the corner to the office of "Harold Dexter, Vice President of Engineering."

Harold was a thin, meek-looking man with a white shirt and tightly knotted blue tie. He rose and offered us his hand. "Hello, gentlemen. Mr. Whitmore told me why you are here and if I can be of any service, please let me know."

Holmes said nothing. I could tell he was taking in Mr. Dexter and his surroundings. His desk, credenza, and bookshelf were occupied by engineering textbooks, handbooks, and no small quantity of bobble-head characters and other paraphernalia from several familiar science fictions and fantasy movies and television shows. Two Star Wars posters hung on the walls. Other odds and ends represented more obscure shows of which I was not familiar.

After an awkward silence, Holmes responded, "Thank you, Mr. Dexter. I shall be in contact if I need anything." With that, he turned and strode back out into the hallway.

I must admit that I was rather nonplussed at my friend's behavior. We had now visited two of the primary suspects and he had asked them nothing. Did he already have reason to believe that one of them was guilty? Or was he more suspicious of the daughter, whose office we were heading towards? I desperately hoped not, for Mr. Whitmore's sake.

Carrie was dressed in more formal business attire than anyone else we had seen at the company. We entered her office and she stood up and walked around her desk to shake hands with each of us.

Holmes said, "Mrs. Sutherland, I suggest on your next cruise to the Bahamas in three weeks, you don't forget to bring your sunscreen like you did last time."

The young lady stopped and looked at my friend with her head cocked and eyes wide.

"Of course, you have a series of pictures on the wall that are clearly taken annually in the Bahamas in front of a Halloween banner with the name of the cruise ship. In the most recent picture, you are clearly sunburnt. And, I noted the airline tickets on your desk. Since Halloween is only three weeks away, I surmised you are continuing your annual tradition."

"Why, yes, Mr. Holmes, I am." She was clearly flustered.

"I'm sorry to have made so personal an observation," Holmes said. This was quite a realization and apology for him, since he is typically quite blind to many of the niceties of British social norms. "Mrs. Sutherland, in your opinion, to what do you attribute the failing finances of your father's company?"

She looked down, then at the ceiling, then at Holmes. "I must agree with my father. Someone is clearly stealing from the company. We're a good company. We do good work and we deliver our products on time. There's no way we can be losing this amount of money."

She moved in closer to Homes and said softly, "I think it's Jurgens, the director of Operations. He's quite capable, but terrible to work with. Always unpleasant. I don't know why, but he must not like my father, so he's driving this dagger into the business, very slowly."

"Thank you, Mrs. Sutherland." Holmes turned to Whitmore. "I believe we have gained enough information today, Mr. Whitmore. You shall be hearing more from us in a few days."

Without waiting for any pleasantries, Holmes strode out of the office and I followed him down the hallway and out the front door.

"Holmes," I exclaimed, "You barely spent 15 minutes in there with the primary suspects! We didn't even get the tour."

"Oh, I have enough information, Watson. I shall make some inquiries on my own and we shall be seeing Mr. Whitmore again soon."

That afternoon, Homes told me that he would be out, possibly for a few days, and to not worry or wait up for him. I have gotten used to his unique methods, but I could not understand how straightforward embezzlement, if there is such a thing, would require my friend to be absent for any length of time. Where could he possibly go? And what would have given him any ideas on how to proceed based on our limited time at the factory? But, sure enough, that afternoon, Holmes left our flat with a backpack on his shoulder, saying nothing other than a perfunctory goodbye.

Three days later, I awoke having heard nothing from Holmes since that last afternoon. As I wearily made my way out from my bedroom to the parlor, I was shocked to nearly run into a strange man standing directly outside my bedroom door. I immediately wished I had my trusty revolver at hand. He was short, stocky, and heavily bearded, wearing overalls covered in dark spots of grime.

"Excuse me!" I blurted. "Who are you? What are you doing in here?"

The man looked at me seriously and then threw his head back and let out a rollicking laugh.

"My dear Watson! You are as constant as the northern star. What great enjoyment I gain from your reactions."

The man, who I then began to recognize as Sherlock Holmes, pulled himself up to his full height and began removing his beard.

"Watson, I have been doing some undercover work at Mr. Whitmore's factory and I believe I have identified the culprit."

"Is it Mr. Jurgens?"

"I shall not name names yet, but I will tell you it is actually two thieves, working in tandem."

"You mean it is Jurgens and Dexter? Surely Mrs. Sutherland can't have anything to do with it, can she?"

Holmes just smiled, then said, "Watson, send a message to Mr. Whitmore and tell him to expect us there shortly. And have him gather his suspects."

"Should we also alert Inspector Lestrade?"

"No, I don't believe that will be necessary."

"Do you mean for the culprits to peacefully give themselves up and go with us to the police station?"

"I don't believe it will come to violence, Watson."

And with that, he grabbed his jacket and deerstalker cap and strode out the door.

We arrived at South London Metalworks and the receptionist escorted us into a conference room. Whitmore was seated at the head of the table with his daughter Carrie at his right side, Dexter to her right, and Jurgens to Whitmore's left.

Holmes walked to the front of the room as if he was about to give a presentation to the CEO. I quietly slipped into a chair along the wall.

"Mr. Whitmore, you do have a thief in your company." Whitmore blanched. This was the moment he was dreading. "And I shall immediately allay your fears. Your daughter has had nothing to do with it."

Whitmore looked relieved. I must admit I was also relieved. But I immediately turned my attention to Mr. Jurgens and Mr. Dexter. Since Holmes said it was two thieves working together, they were the obvious culprits. I wished now that I had brought my revolver or that we had phoned Lestrade. I did not understand why my friend seemed so nonchalant about capturing two embezzlers.

Holmes continued. "Let me also assure you that Mr. Jurgens and Mr. Dexter are also innocent." Everyone looked at each other with obvious relief, which was quickly replaced by confusion.

"Your vice president of engineering, Mr. Dexter, clearly had no motive to embezzle funds from your company. As an engineer, his needs are simple. Engineers are not known for their love of money and he clearly has no social life to speak of that would require great sums. I could see from the decorations in his office if you could call them that, that he would like nothing better on a Saturday night than to watch his favorite science fiction or fantasy movies. He obviously has no interest in illicit gains."

Dexter looked relieved, perturbed, and uncomfortable all at once.

"As for Mr. Jurgens, he deserves a medal for heroism, Mr. Whitmore."

Whitmore said, "Whatever do you mean, sir?"

"Mr. Jurgens has, unbeknownst to himself, been valiantly battling the two embezzlers for the past two years, sometimes achieving daily victories but overall losing the war for the survival of your company. My initial impression of the man was that he was very dedicated to his job. While some may take his gruff exterior for something darker, to me he demonstrated an unwavering dedication to satisfying your customers and keeping the factory working."

"So, who are these criminals, Holmes?" Whitmore exclaimed.

"Over the past few days, I arranged to take employment at your company disguised as a laborer. I must say, my disguise suitably surprised Dr. Watson this morning. But as I observed the factory floor, the culprits became very clear.

"When you said that nothing has changed in the past two years, that was not entirely accurate. You made a sizable investment in a new computer-controlled lathe for machining your products."

"Well, yes, Mr. Holmes. But that was an improvement. We were beginning to reach the limits of our capacity. We purchased it to increase our throughput to better meet our customers' demands and fulfill new orders."

"Unfortunately, the new lathe operated too well. Or, at least, too quickly. It swamped the assembly station that follows it in the production line. It made too many products, too quickly. And, I might add, they did not always fit as they were supposed to."

Whitmore began, "But how…"

"Element…or rather, simple observation. The parts coming from the lathe are stacked up around the assembly station. The assembly station clearly cannot keep up with the output of the lathe. And you can see that many of the parts have been tagged as being non-conforming. So, you are spending a great deal of money on inventory and much of it for parts that are unable to be used."

Jurgens finally piped up. "I told you we didn't need that new-fangled machine. We could have made a few other changes to meet our customer demand."

Whitmore scowled and sat thoughtfully for a moment. "I suppose you were right, Frank. But it seemed like the obvious answer at the time."

Holmes concluded, "Mr. Jurgens is a hero in trying to get product delivered. And I suggest you listen to his recommendations for how to proceed from here."

Whitmore said, "I don't know how to thank you, Mr. Holmes. Now that we know the problem, I think we can recover and get back to making a profit."

"Then with that, Mr. Whitmore, ladies, and gentlemen, Dr. Watson and I will be on our way. Watson, since I am still technically an employee here, what do you say to grab some lunch at the company cafeteria? They serve excellent fish and chips."

7

Manufacturing Planning

"I have another item to add to Manufacturing's TO DO list."

© Cartoon Resource

The Manufacturing Plan

To run the perfect factory, you need the perfect manufacturing plan. Why is this? Why can't you just sort of "do your thing" and have it all come together? In the immortal words of Admiral Painter, the late, great Fred Thompson's character in The Hunt for Red October, "Russians don't **** * **** without a plan." Since this is a family book, I left out the potentially offending language. (Feel free to read "How to Manage the Perfect Factory" to your kids at bedtime. We read Elihu Goldratt's immortal book, The Goal, to our kids on a road trip and they still talk about the "Herbie" to this day. Imagine many years from now your grown kids still talking to you about Manufacturing Readiness Levels and key characteristics! It will warm your heart!) Anyway, you probably know what Fred Thompson was talking about because, if you're a smart person, you've seen Hunt for Red October at least a dozen times. If not, go watch it right now. Or at least look up the quote on the Internet Movie Database.

Fred's message was the Russians were disciplined and organized and they had a plan for everything. Ignore the fact that the Americans won in the end, both in the movie and in real life; the message is still important—you need to have a plan to be successful.

One of the frequently asked questions (a term here which means about three or four people) I get is this: What does the perfect manufacturing plan look like? Do you have an example I can follow?

Once again, in our never-ending effort to help you, dear reader, I have developed a perfect manufacturing plan for you to use. Feel free to copy and paste as much of it as you'd like into your own plan. Chances are your customer has not read this book and will not be suspicious as to the source of your most excellent content. If your customer has read this book, you can exchange knowing glances while respecting each other for fine taste in literature and a well-honed understanding of manufacturing best practices.

Before we get to the example, here are a few tricks of the trade for writing a manufacturing plan.

First, in lieu of having to work hard, be creative, and develop actual details of a manufacturing plan, just restate each of the paragraphs in AS6500 as if that is your plan. Just replace "the organization" with your company's name and the "shalls" with "wills." Here's an example:

AS6500 words:

> *Process Capabilities: The organization shall analyze process capabilities for each critical manufacturing process.*

Turn that into a crisp, direct input for your own manufacturing plan:

> *Process Capabilities: The Airplanes, Inc. Company will analyze process capabilities for each critical manufacturing process.*

Doesn't that sound good? Your management will congratulate you on a fine plan and the customer will be pleased to read such an outstanding passage. The best part is you didn't have to put any work into it at all! What could be better? It's a win-win for everyone. Sure, there aren't any details, but it sounds like you're going to do amazing things! Whether or not you follow through and do what you say you will do is another matter entirely, and we won't concern ourselves with that troublesome detail in this section.

The second trick is to, once again, avoid writing a lot of specific details and only include a list of your company's policies and procedures that are related to each topic. Don't feel like you need to limit yourself to documents that are directly related to each topic, because you're probably getting graded by volume, so throw in as much as you can conceivably include and still be able to sleep with a clear conscience at night. Here's an example of how you can use this technique to enhance the topic we just discussed:

Process Capabilities: The Airplanes, Inc. Company will analyze process capabilities for each critical manufacturing process. We will utilize the following policies and procedures to accomplish this activity:

AS6500 Paragraph	Airplanes, Inc. Process (AIP)
	AIP #2112 Producibility Analysis Procedures
	AIP #2242 Identification of Key Characteristics
	AIP #4243 Development of Annual Budget Inputs
6.2.2 Key Characteristics	AIP #6923 Cleaning and Disinfecting Food Service Items
	Retirement Benefits Calculator
	Intramural soccer schedule
	USA Today

Using these simple techniques will be sure to get your plan approved by your customer, with accolades for you from your management because you were able to do it with such a small budget.

And now, without further ado, here is an example of an ideal manufacturing plan:

MANUFACTURING PLAN FOR THE F-42 AIRCRAFT PROGRAM AIRPLANES, INC

OVERVIEW

1. Introduction:

The Airplanes, Inc. corporation is a multi-national company that is vertically, horizontally, and diagonally integrated to reduce program risk and increase customer satisfaction.

The F-42 aircraft is a multi-use platform that can take off vertically, horizontally, and diagonally to reduce program risk and increase customer satisfaction.

2. Manufacturing Organization:

Airplane Inc's manufacturing organization is top notch. We only hire *summa cum laude* graduates of ivy league universities who spend their free time helping widows and orphans.

The manufacturing organization has clear lines of authority to get the job done. All other organizations respect and bow down to the Director of Manufacturing. When the program is successful, it is due to the incredible efficiency and effectiveness of the Manufacturing organization and all accolades and congratulations should be rendered to the Manufacturing Director. In the unlikely event of program failure, refer to the Directors of Systems Engineering, Finance, and Program Management for root causes of failure.

3. Design Analysis for Manufacturing:

Manufacturing is deeply integrated into the design process. In fact, many of our manufacturing engineers have taken up residence in the homes of the design engineers. Manufacturing and design engineers frequently refer to each other as BFFs and Besties. Per the immortal words of President Ronald

Reagan, we have torn down the wall that typically exists between design and manufacturing. (That is what he was referring to, right?)

3.1 Producibility:

Our company is firmly committed to robust producibility processes that enhance shareholder monetization, corporate synergy, and customer equality.

Our design processes require all the latest tools and techniques for analyzing producibility, including Design for Assembly / Design for Manufacturing, analysis of process capabilities and their ability to meet design tolerances, and the use of automated solid modeling tools to analyze worker ergonomics.

In addition to these proven best practices, our company has pioneered a new approach to analyzing producibility. We call it, "Special Techniques Using Politicians In Design" or by the acronym, STUPID. In other words, "Can a politician put this design together?" We decided to go to the lowest common denominator of individual intelligence and capability to design our manufacturing processes to be truly idiot proof. We began by using actual politicians to test our work instructions but found them to be too expensive and they were frequently caught stealing office supplies. Since then, we have programmed a special artificial intelligence program (although in this case, it is an artificial dis-intelligence program) to model the buffoonery of the politicians. This has highlighted numerous instances where work instructions have been confusing, especially in highly technical process steps like, "Insert tab A into slot B."

Out STUPID program will ensure the F-42 aircraft can be easily manufactured by literally anyone.

Our program managers clearly support STUPID initiatives.

Finance managers have also agreed to provide funding for STUPID activities.

When it comes to supplier participation in producibility studies, they are also on board with STUPID.

3.2 Key Characteristics

Despite what OTHER companies say, we LOVE key characteristics. In fact, not only do we identify key characteristics on the product, we identify them in other areas of the company as well. Here are some examples:

Area	Key Characteristic Examples
Engineering	Thickness of each design change package
	Number of pens and pencils per pocket protector
	Number of ties worn with short sleeve shirts
Cafeteria	Volume of each serving of mystery slop per lunch tray
	Number of napkins required per person on Taco Tuesday
Janitorial Services	Hours per day with empty paper towel dispensers in restrooms
	Number of rolls of toilet paper required on Taco Tuesday

4. Manufacturing Readiness Levels

Manufacturing Readiness Levels (MRLs) are a way of life at Airplanes Inc. On the F-42 program, we analyzed thousands of processes and suppliers. We assessed every internal process, including final assembly, subassembly, composite fabrication, machining, paper towel replacement process in the restrooms, mimeograph machine copying, parking lot restriping, and snack bar restocking.

We are pleased to report that each and every one of the thousands of processes are at an MRL of 10, the highest level possible. We realize that some companies just claim to be at MRL 10 for purely political purposes. However, we assure you that we really are at MRL 10 everywhere. You can trust us.

We also assessed our 10,000 first and second tier suppliers and they, too, are at MRL 10. The only exception is Fred's Autobody and Aerospace Structures Technologies. They are at MRL 1, the lowest possible score, but we have a plan in place to rapidly get them to a 10 in 45 days. Trust us.

Despite being at MRL 10 in all areas, the assessments never-the-less identified some significant risks to the program. These risks include:

→ Clueless program managers
→ Chinese hackers
→ Food poisoning
→ Eruption of the Yellowstone Caldera

We have developed effective Manufacturing Risk Reduction Plans for each of these that reduce the risk to Low, except for the Program Managers. We continue to carry this as a high risk.

Manufacturing Schedule

Below are the major events in our time-phased, event-based schedule, estimated in months after contract award (MACA):

Contract Award = 0

Facility construction and modification = 1 MACA

Release purchase orders for long lead items = 1 MACA

Release work orders for internal part fabrication = 1 MACA

Release major tooling design to tooling fabrication organization = 1 MACA

Complete rough design of the product = 12 MACA

Revise and rework facility construction and modification = 13 MACA

Revise purchase orders for long lead items = 13 MACA

Revise work orders for internal part fabrication and begin reworking parts = 13 MACA

Revise major tooling design and rework tools = 13 MACA

Complete final design of the product = 24 MACA

Revise and rework facility construction and modification = 25 MACA

Revise purchase orders for long lead items = 25 MACA

Revise work orders for internal part fabrication and begin reworking parts = 25 MACA

Revise major tooling design and rework tools = 25 MACA

(While this early development schedule may seem inefficient with numerous reworking of parts and tooling, it is fully compliant with the contract and achieves all contract incentives to begin manufacturing work as soon as possible. In addition, all of these activities are allowable charges, so shareholder equity will be maximized and the actual costs can be used in cost projections for future program.)

Completion of first development aircraft = 36 MACA

Production Decision = 36 MACA

First Flight = 37 MACA

Completion of software development = 48 MACA

(While this schedule may have some risk inherent in it due to the fact that a production decision must be made prior to even flying the first development aircraft, have no fear. This is standard operating procedure in the government acquisition world and rumor has it that no program has ever been denied a production decision just because of a little thing called "concurrency risk.")

[As a side note for those readers in the automotive industry or other civilian, consumer product industries, the Department of Defense often plans its programs with a significant amount of concurrency. Parts and subassemblies for developmental units are expected to be produced even before the overall design is complete and production begins while testing is still ongoing. If this approach were used in any other industry, heads would explode at the level of risk and almost guaranteed level of rework. As Mr. Scott, the Chief Engineer of the USS Enterprise said, "I can't change the laws of physics!" Well, apparently, the federal government can. Or at least, they've got the deep pockets to suck up the impacts of all those changes and rework.]

6. Modeling and Simulation

Airplane, Inc. utilizes the latest and greatest software tools to model the anticipated production processes and factory layouts to ensure it will meet the capacity requirements of the current and future contracts and identify bottlenecks and problems early enough in the development process to allow time to mitigate their effects. Our marketing department worked long and hard on the preceding sentence, so we hope you enjoyed it.

Our modeling and simulation subject matter experts are fluent in the most current digital environments and tools, including Fortnite, Legend of Zelda, Mario Cart, and Minecraft. Our planned production facility was constructed virtually in Minecraft and we can assure the customer that it is sufficiently protected from Creepers, Zombies, Skeletons, and Endermen. (Ask your kids if you don't know what these are).

7. Unique Manufacturing Technology.

We will be making use of 3D printing and Additive Manufacturing techniques. Additive Manufacturing and 3D printing figure prominently in our value stream and our advertisements. We will extensively utilize both of those terms in as much of our literature as possible because they are the latest buzzwords that get the most attention from program managers who know nothing about them or their significant limitations. But all program mangers want to be on the cutting edge and be able to say they are doing "that stuff." Did we mention we will be using 3D printing and Additive Manufacturing yet? Feel free to assign bonus points now.

Anticipated F-42 parts to be fabricated using 3D printing and additive manufacturing:

→ Cockpit cupholder (Note, this is no ordinary cupholder. It is required to hold the 40 ounce Super Big Chugger Cup which normal production tooling cannot accommodate, hence the need for 3D printing.)
→ Miniature F-42 models suitable for attaching to key chains and handing out at conferences and other marketing events.
→ Structural components for the rear-view mirror.
→ The little switch that fades the on-board FM stereo from the front seat to the rear seat.

8. Facilities

Using our modeling and simulation capabilities, we have properly sized our facility to handle all the anticipated workload throughout the life of the F-42 program. Our facility includes sufficient floorspace and utilities for:

→ Final Assembly
→ Metal machining
→ Composite Fabrication
→ 3D Printing
→ Additive Manufacturing
→ Water slides

→   Bowling Alley
→   Day spa, featuring massage tables, saunas, and poker tables (for the exclusive use of program managers)

9. Manufacturing Processes

To avoid overly detailed and possible proprietary and classified information, a simplified process flow for the F-42 aircraft program is described as follows: First, we build little parts. These are then attached to each other to make bigger parts. Finally, they are attached to make a really big part. Then those really big parts are screwed, clipped, and glued together to make an airplane. Then we make sure all the lights come on, and then we put gas in and fly it.

10. Manpower

Using the latest modeling and simulation techniques, we forecasted our manpower needs, time-phased throughout the program and by each unique skill set. Acquiring sufficiently skilled manpower in a timely manner is often a program risk and is impacted by the availability of a ready, trained workforce. That's why we have tailored our recruiting approach to be flexible, based on the robustness of the national economy.

If the economy is weak and people are desperate for jobs, we anticipate no problems in hiring highly educated people into minimum wage jobs. On the other hand, if the economy is strong, our plan is to lower our standards and recruit at local prisons, car dealers, and government offices.

11. Productivity Improvement

The key to affordability is to ensure a productive workforce. Here at Airplanes, Inc, we utilize the latest strategies to ensure we get the most out of our workforce, including:

→   Encouraging a healthy workforce by replacing the potato chips and candy bars in the vending machines with apples and kale.
→   Reducing unnecessary time in the restrooms by eliminating modern plumbing and installing outhouses in the field behind the factory. This program has been especially successful in our Minot, North Dakota, division.
→   Using motivational posters. Some of the most popular slogans include: "I've seen your grandma working harder than what you're

doing right now," "Don't be a lazy sow; be a hard worker now," and "Roses are red, violets are blue, if you don't work harder, we'll fire you."

Unfortunately, due to recent OSHA regulations and court orders, we were forced to eliminate our "No Slacking Off Shock Collar Program."

12. Labor Relations

Here at Airplanes, Inc, we have a fine union representing our hardworking employees. We believe the union fosters trust, partnership, and loyalty between its members and company management. The union also ensures that each member is conscientious and diligent in the work they perform. The comradery between union and management could not be better.

The last time a strike occurred (three years ago), Airplane, Inc management acknowledged they were engaged in unfair labor practices and the union was 100% in the right.

We love our union.*

*The preceding statements are required by union agreement 19-AIC-9299929 and does not reflect the views of Airplane, Inc corporation management.

13. Subcontractor/Supplier Management

The first step of our supplier management process is to determine if the part should be produced in-house or at a supplier. To do this, we perform a thorough Make/Buy analysis, taking into account such factors as our strategic goals, internal capabilities and capacities, cost of make vs buy, kickback opportunities with "friendly" suppliers, and the difficulty to produce the product internally (better to blame a supplier than our own company if there are problems.)

Once a decision has been made to off-load a part, we conduct a rigorous process to ensure a top-notch, high quality, affordable supplier is selected. To manage suppliers, we:

→ Flow down cost, schedule, and performance requirements to suppliers and provide timely notification of changes.

→ Continually assess overall health of the supplier management organization.

→ Identify and manage supplier risks, such as quality, technical, schedule, long-lead times, and financial health.

→ Identify approved (qualified) suppliers and periodically re-assess qualification.

In addition, we would never, ever, just mindlessly copy the preceding words from the AS6500 standard into our manufacturing plan.

14. Process Control Plans

Typical process control plans are usually just warmed-over work instructions with no special considerations for reducing variation. Our process control plans aim to get to the true root cause of variation in processes. For example:

If a Key Characteristic of a machined part is a certain dimension, we ask, "what impacts that dimension?" We may find that the capability of the machine and the cutting tool impacts that dimension and they have limits as to what tolerances they can hold. But we aren't satisfied to stop there.

We then ask, "What impacts the capability of the machine?" In this example, we found that, due to the limitations of machining technology and variation in materials, bearings, drive mechanisms, and fixtures, there are limits to how precise a machine can be.

But we still weren't satisfied. We continued to ask why this is so. After completing a fishbone diagram, we discovered we can only control so much and that variation is due to the Biblical concept of original sin, a fallen creation, and the Total Depravity of man. Now that the great reformer and theologian John Calvin has helped us to identify the true root cause, we can develop an appropriate process control plan. In this case, the steps in the process control plan are: (1) Pray for grace and mercy. (2) Repeat.

15. Summary

In conclusion, this manufacturing plan will result in products delivered ahead of schedule, under budget, and with quality that will make your eyes water.

Supply Chain and Material Management

DMSMS

Diminishing Manufacturing Sources and Material Shortages. Back in the old days, we used to just call these "obsolete parts." Now, with the new term, we call it DMSMS. A nice acronym is always an improvement. However, this is not a nice acronym because it doesn't make a fun word, so it's clearly not an improvement.

Much like late and bad engineering, DMSMS will prevent you from maintaining the perfectly run factory. And much like bad engineering, it's not your fault! But here's the frustrating thing: Because that lousy acronym has the word "Manufacturing" in its title, everyone thinks the Manufacturing Engineer is responsible. That's not fair. It's really Engineering's fault for specifying a part with the lifespan of a fruit fly. And it's Procurement's fault for not proactively managing their suppliers and forecasting when parts will no longer be made. So, you are completely off the hook. Whew.

Not exactly. Your leadership will still look to YOU to fix these problems before they impact deliveries. Fortunately, after reading this book, you will know the secret solution to avoiding DMSMS impacts: Are you ready? Money. Lots of it. Bucket loads. Do you know how people say that money doesn't buy happiness? It does here. If you have bucket loads of money, you can spend it on forecasting tools and industry surveys to determine early enough when a part is going obsolete. Then you can buy a lifetime supply of those parts. Or you can redesign the item that the obsolete part goes into and make it even better. All you need is money. There is a well-proven correlation: The programs with the most money to spend on DMSMS have the least impacts. How simple is that?

Counterfeit parts are a closely related issue to DMSMS because when parts go obsolete, engineers may have a challenge finding a replacement part. They may be so desperate that they go to "Bob's Distributor of Fine Electronic Devices and Sushi" which promises they still have a supply of the needed component, even though it was made in Guandong Province in China.

I have the solution to all the counterfeit electronic part problems: Bring back the good old Radio Shack stores! Remember those? You could buy all sorts of electronic kits and parts. It was like a toy store for future engineers. I'm sure we could build an Active Electronically Scanned Array Radar system out of those myriads of parts they had mounted on the walls in the local Radio Shack located in your nearest shopping mall. Ah, the good old days.

"This machine literally does nothing except fold paper into paper airplanes."

Cost

Engineers, when confronted with questions of cost, will usually respond by frantically shrieking, "Run away! Run away!" And then they do.

But the perfect factory implies that it is actually making money. That's why your company hired you. You may think they care about your welfare and they want every member of your family to have a new smartphone, season tickets to the nearest NFL team, and braces for little Suzie's imperfect teeth, but they really just love you for the money you can earn for them.

And guess what? Not to side with "The Man," "The Oppressor," or "The Bourgeoisie," but they are right. But in a good way. You, a shining example of the Proletariat, and a true Manufacturing/Quality/Supplier Management subject matter expert, have an incredible influence over the profitability of your company.

How much influence on cost do other functions have?

Design engineers (or the "Engineers from the Dark Side" as we discussed earlier) have the most impact on how much a product costs because, well, they designed it. They may not have designed it well, but they designed it. We can help them do better.

What about program managers, who are ultimately responsible for everything? Yes, they are responsible, but they don't actually do anything. Really, their job is to just nag everyone else to do better and do it cheaper. All that nagging is just nibbling around the fringes of cost.

How about the Accounting and Finance people? It seems they have a big role, but they just sign the checks. They don't make the product any cheaper. Although I do appreciate that they sign my paycheck, so maybe we should just ignore what I just said.

How about Personnel/Human Resources? Since we're all just an HR Specialist's keystroke away from being assigned to Pothole, Alabama (no offense intended for Alabama-ites. I'm sure the rest of the state is just fine), we'll leave out any negative words for HR, too, except to say that they really don't drive the cost of the product either.

Which leaves you. What can you do to improve profitability for your company? This is not just a hypothetical question. It's actually a simple quiz.

Quiz: What can I do to improve profitability for my company?

☑ a. Resign.

☑ b. Stop screwing up.

☑ c. Take raw materials home and build some products in my garage on my own time.

☑ d. Effectively implement all the time-tested best practices of SAE's standard for Manufacturing Management, AS6500.

Scoring: If you answered:

a or b: Tender your resignation now. It's probably better that you not be in the workforce if this answer is true. Supporting you with food stamps may be a better long-term investment by the taxpayers for the future of our country than having you working and making a mess of things.

c: Take 5 bonus points. Your company appreciates your willingness to donate your own time and home for the benefit of their bottom line. Hopefully, though, your company's product is not a weapon of mass destruction. The neighbors might be upset if something goes wrong.

d: Congratulations! You are either extremely smart or you're sly enough to know that this is just like when you were in Sunday School and anyone who answered "Jesus" was never wrong.

The Learning Curve

Now let's get into the nuts and bolts of cost estimating. This is where we encounter everyone's friend, the learning curve. Of course, ivory tower purists call it the "improvement curve" because more factors go into improvement than just operator learning. But since we're not ivory tower purists, let's delve into the learning curve.

The basic theory of the learning curve is that, as you double the quantity of an item produced, the time to produce it is reduced by a constant rate. For example, if it takes 100 hours to assemble the first unit and it takes 80 hours to assemble the second unit, we say it is on an 80% learning curve. If this curve continues, unit 4 (which is double unit two) will take 80% of unit 2, or 64 hours. If we double the units again from 4 to 8, then we take 80% of 64 to get....well, I don't have a calculator handy, but you get the idea.

You may have encountered this phenomenon in your personal life. I noticed this effect when I changed the oil in my car. I got better and faster at it over time until I cut the time down to ZERO and neglected to change the oil at all because I was too busy. One pricy ring job later and I learned to just take it to Quicky Lube, whose employees are way down the learning curve already (or not), but you pay as if they're always on the first unit.

Since you are running the perfect factory and have implemented an amazing producibility program and air-tight process controls, your first unit is going to be produced as perfectly and efficiently as humanly possible. In the language of learning curves, this means that you will be on a 100% learning curve because every unit after the first unit will take the same time to produce since there is no inefficiency to eliminate.

However, you don't want to rub peoples' noses in your perfection. And the customer won't like it if you tell them you're not including a learning curve in your cost estimates. They may find it hard to believe that you are running at such a level of perfection. So, just to make them feel better, throw in a little inefficiency upfront and tell them you'll give them a 90% improvement curve. They won't like that because they will say it's too flat, so go ahead and throw in some more inefficiency and give them an 80% curve. This may satisfy them. But if you truly want to exceed the customer expectations, go wild with your inefficiencies. Assign the laziest employees, write the work instructions in Klingon (unless your workers are all Star Trek nerds who actually know the Klingon language), throw a wrench (literally) into the machine, and give your suppliers design tolerances that you could drive a truck through. Then tell your customer you will come down a 70% curve. They will be ecstatic.

Let's say you've effectively included some inefficiencies or (God forbid) you're working in a factory that isn't perfect yet. And let's say you are really coming down a 70% learning curve. What do you tell people? Certainly not the truth!

Here's a handy little guide on what to tell each stakeholder when they ask what curve you are forecasting:

What to tell your employees: 65%
- After all, you want them to always feel they're not working hard enough.

What to tell your boss: 75%
- Now you have a nice little buffer to be sure to earn your annual bonus.

What to tell the Finance Manager: 85%
- You'll find plenty of things to do with that extra budget, right? And you'll be a hero for coming in under budget, even if you've sprung for that big screen tv in your office and season tickets to the Met.

What to tell the customer: 95%
- Of course, they won't be happy, but if you can get them to pay for a 95% learning curve, you may also be able to sell them a certain bridge in a certain city.

Manufacturing Modeling & Simulation (M&S)

Running the perfect factory requires smart, computer-savvy engineers. Sadly, this is not me. If you needed something done in FORTRAN, I could have done that about 30 years ago. This is probably not you, either. If it was, you'd probably be making twice the salary you are now and be enjoying perks like free massages, lattes, and ping pong tables.

Here's a test to see if you're too old to run M&S programs yourself: I recently took a class in a very cool factory modeling and simulation software package. It was amazingly powerful. I followed along just fine in the class; I wasn't lost at all, which made me feel very proud of myself. And I even had a project that I needed to apply it to, so I was very excited about getting started with the software. The problem was, after the class, I did nothing with it the next week. I came back the following week and pretty much forgot everything I knew. If this happens to you, it's time to admit you have an old age problem and need to just go ahead and hire some hotshot kid fresh out of college. They might not know every software language or M&S package out there, but that's what Google is for. Seriously, these whippersnappers can learn new languages and software just by Googling everything they need to be able to code. It makes me mad and they need to get off my lawn!

The textbook answer for why to use M&S is: you can make mistakes in an electronic model before you actually make expensive mistakes with a poor manufacturing layout. But the real reason for using M&S is: you can make mistakes in an electronic model before you actually make expensive mistakes with a poor manufacturing layout. Sometimes the textbooks are right.

Manufacturing Workforce

If you are reading this book during a strong economy, my condolences. Yes, business is probably going well for you, you're making wheelbarrows full of money every day, and customers can't get enough of your product. But your biggest challenge may be the workforce. That darned good economy means that you must compete for the best workers. Finding good employees and keeping them is especially hard in this environment. A good economy and low unemployment are banes to your perfect factory. All the good workers are taken!

If you're reading this book during a weak economy, congratulations! You may be about to go bankrupt and barely able to replace the hand towels in the bathroom, but at least you have many qualified candidates knocking on your door asking for a job! As a bonus, you don't even have to pay them much! Just offer them minimum wage and throw in a $25 McDonald's gift card as a signing bonus and you're good to go. A suffering country is good for you!

No matter which economy you find yourself in, finding the right workers is always a challenge for running the perfect factory. Part of your problem may be how you screen potential employees. You may be too strict in your screening process or you may be too lenient. That's why our crack research staff has compiled a list of common mistakes.

If you are asking questions like these, you may be too strict:

1. Will you pledge your first-born child to the service of the company?
2. Are you satisfied with a salary that includes only a daily bag of tree nuts, a head of lettuce, and clean underwear?
3. When not at work, why aren't you at work?
4. Do you maintain a rigorous exercise regimen to ensure your fitness for performing your job?
5. Have you ever, or will you ever, make a mistake?

On the flip side, the following questions may indicate that you are too lax in your standards and desperate for employees:

1. Do you limit your illegal drug use to evenings, lunches, and coffee-breaks?
2. Is your pulse mostly existent?
3. Do you pledge to not attack your supervisor with a knife, gun, machete, or broken beer bottle when he or she asks why you missed the last week of work without calling in?
4. Do you renounce your allegiance to ISIS?
5. Were at least 50% of your felonies non-violent?

© SAE International

Once you navigate the initial screening process, then you must kick it into gear and really determine if a candidate is right for you. Instead of the typical interview questions, many social media and high-tech employers have moved to ask outside-the-box thinking and problem-solving questions to gain insight into a prospective employee's ability to think quickly under stress.

Here are some of the old interview questions and why it no longer makes send to use them:

1. What is your greatest strength? (Most frequent answer: I work too hard.)
2. What is your greatest weakness? (Most frequent answer: I work too hard.)
3. What is your greatest accomplishment? Most frequent answer: I worked too hard and saved my last company $10 Million, but they went out of business anyway.)

© SAE International

Here are some newer, better questions asked by the forward-thinking companies:

1. If you were a mold spore, what kind of mold spore would you be? Be specific.

2. If you were in a raft and had to take the Queen of England, Donald Trump, and Bernie Sanders across a river one at a time, who would you throw overboard first?

3. In five minutes or less, create a JAVA program to calculate how many graviton pulses per second would be required to excite 10 grams of antimatter to accelerate the Millennium Falcon to one point five hyperspace speed. Be sure to include as part of your answer why Star Wars ignores all rules of physics.

These questions are sure to give you the employees you deserve.

8

Manufacturing Operations Management

"WE NEED SOMEONE TO GET US BEYOND PQM.
PARTIAL QUALITY MANAGEMENT."

© Cartoon Resource

If you're in a desperate situation with your factory, just think back to the book "The Goal" by Eliyahu Goldratt. You may remember the beleaguered plant manager in that story, Alex Rogo. Actually, he had it easy. Yes, he was going to lose his job, his family, and his reputation, but at least he had his old professor and guru, Jonah, to help him. Sadly, you've got no one like a Jonah in your life to swoop in to give you sage advice on how to turn things around when things look the darkest. Oh, wait! Yes, you do! Now you have AS6500! It's like your own personal Jonah guru. And it's better than Jonah because it has the wit and wisdom of a crew of industry experts to guide you. So, take that, Mr. Goldratt!

Actually, if you haven't read his book, you should. As they have said in several Star Trek episodes, his exploits were required reading at the academy. As I mentioned before, we read "The Goal" to our kids when they were young (yes, we are an incredibly nerdy family. I even taught my kids, process flow diagrams when they were about 8 years old. And I taught them about Schrodinger's Cat. And the Second Law of Thermodynamics, to which my youngest daughter responded, "So, why bother cleaning my room if entropy is just going to increase anyway?) So, if you haven't read it yet, put down this book immediately and read The Goal. (You've already paid for this book, so I don't mind if you don't actually finish reading it.)

Continuous Improvement

Based on the number of books available on continuous improvement, quality, and other management fads, every factory that employs a literate workforce should be the perfect factory. And what about all those colleges that teach continuous improvement concepts and techniques? With all that knowledge so readily available, why isn't every factory the perfect factory? Can people really not read? Are all the books wrong? Or have they just been prematurely consigned to the bargain book bin at the local used book stores? Are college professors wrong? The answers to these questions are no, no, maybe, and maybe.

Fortunately, this book is DIFFERENT! It will never be in the clearance aisle at Barnes and Noble. But that's because Barnes and Nobel probably won't even buy any copies in the first place. Can you say, "niche marketing?"

But this book is clearly different from all the other continuous improvement books because … the words "continuous," "improvement," "quality," "sigma," or "free" don't appear in the title.

However, all the continuous improvement elements that work together to bring you manufacturing bliss have been very helpfully collected in AS6500.

The history of continuous improvement is littered with fads and failures. What's your favorite? Who remembers Total Quality Management (TQM)? Or "TQM" as it was called? "TQM" ended up being far too long of an acronym, so it was later shortened to just "TQ." Much better.

TQ ended up trying to be all things to all people, ala "What would help you do your job better?" For the organization I was in, we decided that (1) the mail could be delivered to our desks quicker and (2) we needed a pop (or soda, if you're not from around here) machine. To attack the mail situation, we came up with a process to timestamp the mail as soon as it arrived in our office. Then the secretary (remember those?) would timestamp it each time it moved from location to location. Once you received a piece of mail, you were supposed to enter the time you received it into a log. This project died a rapid death due to lack of interest. I think it even died before the first piece of timestamped mail reached its intended recipient. We also never got a pop machine. We didn't get a soda machine, either.

Then there was an explosion of continuous improvement initiatives: Lean, Six Sigma, Lean Six Sigma, Kaizen, Standardized Work, the Toyota Production System, Just-In-Time Manufacturing, Theory of Constraints, Advanced Product Quality Planning, and Define/Measure/Analyze/Improve/Control. If we combine all of these into one acronym, we get LSSLSSKSWTPSJITToCAPQPDMAIC. And you thought the LGBTQ community had a long acronym! This combined continuous improvement acronym really embodies intersectionality.

Each of these has their strengths and weaknesses.

Continuous Improvement Initiative

Lean

Strength: It sounds healthy, like Lean Cuisine.

Weakness: Just like healthy food, it might not taste as good.

Six Sigma

Strength: Very mathy.

Weakness: Very mathy.

Lean Six Sigma

Strength: Whoever came up with this was brilliant. It didn't require anything new, just combining two existing initiatives. Like Reese's Peanut Butter cups.

Weakness: Lots of people have been trained in this, but does anyone ever USE it? (I was at a company that was having quality issues and, to get to the conference room, I walked past dozens of cubicles. The nameplates posted on those cubes had "Six Sigma Certified" under their names. So, why were they having quality problems???)

Kaizen

Strength: Seems to work well.

Weakness: Hard to spell.

Standardized Work

Strength: Makes lots of sense—variation is the enemy of manufacturing.

Weakness: It takes a lot of work!

The Toyota Production System

Strength: Hey, it's Toyota!

Weakness: Unable to comment due to threat from Toyota lawyers.

Just-In-Time Manufacturing

Strength: Makes your factory look really good and uncluttered.

Weakness: Since this is really just a subset of the Toyota Production System, if you don't do the whole TPS thing, you'll find yourself frequently being short of parts. The uncluttered look can be bad when you need to produce 10,000 items a day and one of your suppliers missed their daily delivery.

continues

continued

<u>Theory of Constraints</u>
Strength: Based on a really cool book.
Weakness: The book was better than the initiative.

<u>Advanced Product Quality Planning</u>
Strength: Hey, it's from the automotive industry, so it must be good.
Weakness: Every other industry says, "That doesn't apply to us."

<u>Define/Measure/Analyze/Improve/Control</u>
Strength: Pretty mathy.
Weakness: Hey, is this a Six Sigma rip-off?

In this list of continuous improvement initiatives, I did not list Deming's 14 points, because, you don't mess with Deming. His ideas are bigger than just making process improvements. The Master is not to be mocked.

Metrics

I'm often asked, "What are the right metrics for measuring how well my factory is performing?" Metrics can be a tricky topic.

I know that you run a perfect factory.

You know that you run a perfect factory.

But the metrics that your CEO sees might not reflect the reality in your head. So, here are a few common metrics with some tips to make sure they tell the story that YOU want to tell and ensure they make you shine.

Scrap/Rework/Repair (SRR): Ideally, you want this to be zero, or at least show a steep downward trend since the day you started on the job. If you're in a tight situation, the best approach is to change the definition of what's in each of the numbers. For example, if the numbers aren't looking good, but they've got all your overhead included in the dollar values (something we like to call "burdened"), simply change the numbers to "unburdened." Strip out all the overhead and, viola, a nice big step down in SRR. You're a hero! You can also fiddle around with whichever looks best: raw numbers or percentages of some bigger number, like labor costs. Raw numbers might hit too close to home, but if your SRR is 5% of labor costs, that doesn't sound so bad. And then you can start with unburdened labor costs as the denominator of that percentage until that gig is up, then make them burdened! Once again, a big step down and you're a hero again. Feel free to move other cost centers in and out of that base, just to keep things coming down that curve.

Numbers of Nonconformances: Much like SRR, the key to managing this metric is to change the definitions when things are looking grim. One very helpful approach is to change from the number of non-conformances to the number of non-conforming items. Do you see what that does? If you had a single part with 57 holes misdrilled, the number 57 doesn't look so good on your chart. But, hey, it was only "One item" that was non-conforming, right? One looks much better than 57. And most program managers aren't smart enough to appreciate the difference between nonconformances and nonconforming items.

And then there's always the trick of tracking the number of non-conformances per "opportunity of non-conformances." Man, that's just a made-up number! Have fun with that one! You can say that you had 57 nonconformances out of 10 million opportunities! Talk about Six Sigma material!

Out of Station Work: While this might look bad for you, don't forget these delays are ALWAYS driven by late parts from suppliers. And that's not your fault. So, when you show this metric, never show it alone. Always include ON THAT CHART a list of the late parts that are causing you headaches. Then turn to the Director of Supplier Management and ask him what he's doing about it. That's like a ninja moves to deflect the incoming attacks.

Efficiency or Realization: First a little background. Efficiency is the ratio of the standard hours (or hours that a task should take in a perfect world) divided by the actual hours that it took to perform. For example, if a task should take 50 hours, but it actually took 100 hours, then the factory was 50/100 or 50% efficient. Realization is just the inverse of that. It is the actual hours divided by the standard hours or, in this example, 100 actual hours/50 standard hours result in a realization factor of 2.

What is a good number for these values? Hypothetically, the perfect factory would be at 100% efficiency or a 1.0 Realization Factor. But there are reasons why you might not want to report those ideal results. First, it might raise eyebrows. Even though you have told the world that you are running the perfect factory, when the CEO repeatedly sees 100% efficiency, he might get suspicious. You want to make it look good, but not too good. In this case, something like 97% efficiency sure sounds pretty good. It's believable and impressive, but not too suspicious, especially if you vary it by a few percentage points each month.

Another strategy is to show a lower (but not too low) efficiency, maybe in the upper 80s or so. This gives you the opportunity to earn big annual bonuses by constantly nudging those numbers closer to 100%.

To make this metric look good, the actual hours are hard to fudge. Your real targets of opportunity are those "standard hours." After all, who really knows what that means? No one knows how those standard hours were created or what's in them other than you and maybe a few of your paid underling Planners or Industrial Engineers. As a result, the easiest thing in the world to do is to multiple your standard hours by some factor to give you the efficiency you want and deserve.

Here's a handy example:

$$\text{Actual hours} = 100$$
$$\text{Standard hours} = 50$$
$$\text{Desired efficiency} = 95\%$$
$$.95 = (50 \text{ standard hours}) \times (X \text{ factor}) / (100 \text{ actual hours})$$
$$\text{Solving for } X = .95 \,(100) / 50 = 1.9$$

Therefore, multiply all your standard hours by a factor of 1.9 (and this factor does NOT have to appear prominently in any calculations, wink, wink) and, congratulations, you are now running a factory that is 95% efficient.

If you're casting around for a good factor, Pi seems like an elegant, engineering number. Feel free to use it.

By the way, if you think this entire discussion on multiplying standards by a factor to get the desired efficiency sounds just a little too improbable (no one would actually do that, right?), I'm here to tell you that I've actually seen it done. After all, that's how I got the idea to put it in this book. Truth is stranger than fiction. I will not name names, but you know who you are!

Line of Balance: Fortunately, only old, grey-beards will remember this metric and how it should really be constructed. The foundation of the metric is a process flow chart with critical inventory control points identified. It includes a schedule of how many units should have passed through each control point based on the scheduled demand and set back/span times for each step in the process. The focus of the metric is a chart showing the number of units that have actually passed through each of those points compared with how many should have passed through them.

Avoid this metric at all costs! It's far too insightful and nearly impossible to game. It has the added unpleasantness of forecasting how far behind you will be in the future. And no one wants to see that.

If your customer insists on seeing a line of balance metric, your only hope is to do what some companies have done: Use a Gantt chart to show each unit's progress through the factory (and you may even draw a crooked line through where they "should" be, but this is highly subjective and no one is going to be able to verify where your line is supposed to be. So, draw that chart and slap a "Line of Balance" title on there and call it good!

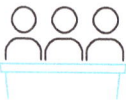

Engineering Changes: This metric is your best friend! Anytime you get criticized for cost, quality, or schedule problems, whip out this metric and tell everyone, "Yes, we're behind schedule, but just look at the volume of engineering changes we've had to deal with. If those darn engineers would just stop making changes, we could really be pumping this product out the door." This metric helps you blame an imperfect factory back where it truly belongs: with the Engineers from the Dark Side.

You must be careful, however, to avoid showing any long-term trends that might indicate that the current magnitude of changes is minuscule compared to the past. Here's where you must pick only the most recent data and then adjust the Y-axis accordingly so that even two or three changes per month show a bar graph that stretches the entire height of the paper.

First-Pass Yields: This is the world's easiest metric to fudge. After all, the term "first pass" is really in the eye of the beholder. What does "first" really mean? What is the meaning of "is?" If running a part through an acceptance test procedure multiple times is "expected," then that's all the justification you need to count two failures followed by a pass as 100% first-pass yield. If someone presses you on this approach, just call it, "planned adjustments" or say the first two "failures" were really just "tuning."

Quality Escapes: This is another one of those metrics that could get ugly for you and take the shine off your perfect factory. If quality escapes are an issue, you could try to blame the Quality organization, but some forward-thinking intellectual will probably point out that "quality is everyone's responsibility."

Probably your best bet is to show zero quality escapes on this metric, no matter what so-called-reality says. The definitional jujitsu is this: If a quality problem was found by your customer, then "The system" – defined VERY broadly – worked, right? After all, your customer is really part of the team. They're part of the enterprise, too. In other words, they are part of "The System" to catch quality problems. When it all comes down to it, what REALLY is a "quality escape? Engaging in this philosophical debate may be just enough of a distraction to allow you to move on to the next chart.

Variability Reduction (VR)

When talking about Variability Reduction (VR), most people just assume it means Statistical Process Control (SPC), but VR is a larger mindset and includes the use of SPC as well as process control plans. By the way, Variability Reduction used the acronym VR long before Virtual Reality was a thing.

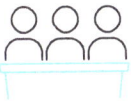

The foundation of VR is the Taguchi Loss Function. And with a name like "Taguchi Loss Function" the concept of VR has instant credibility. I've even thrown this concept around in front of Engineers from the Dark Side and they looked as if they were almost ready to consider me a "real" engineer.

The Taguchi Loss Function states that the further away from the design nominal a given characteristic is, the larger the cost will be to society. See the graph below. Earlier in this book, we actually used math to calculate factory efficiency; now we're using graphs. I bet you didn't realize what you were getting into. AS6500 really makes you work!

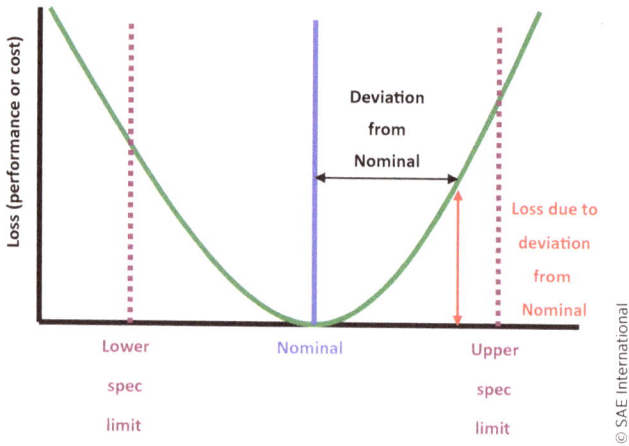

© SAE International

In my expert interpretation of the Taguchi Loss Function, in applying it to the factory environment, we can say the farther away a characteristic is from the design nominal, the more it will cost either the factory (in scrap, rework, repair, shimming, making it fit, etc.) or the customer (how soon it will wear out, break, or degrade in performance).

The idea of VR is to reduce the output of a process to be as repeatedly close to the design nominal as possible. This is in contrast to the typical mindset that says anything within the design tolerance is good and acceptable. We call this the goal post mentality. In looking at the figure below, if a given measurement (X1) is at the nominal, we consider that to be very good. If it is outside of the specification limits (X2), then it is deemed to be "bad." But if it is just inside the design tolerance (X3), then it is deemed to be "good." But the "good" measurement X3 is actually closer to the "bad" measurement X2 than it is to the very good measurement, X1, which is at the design nominal. It's only that hairsbreadth difference around the upper specification limit that keeps it from being "bad." As Mr. Spock would say, this is "Highly illogical."

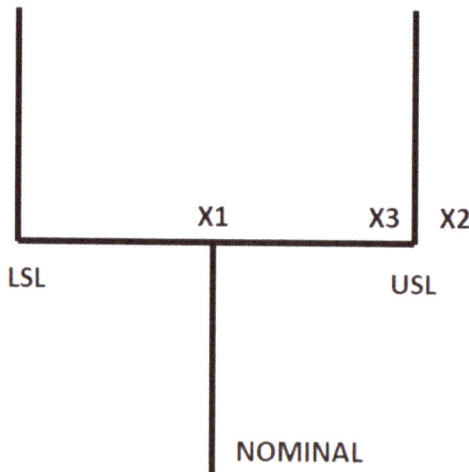

© SAE International

The rallying cry of VR is to eliminate the "Goal Post Mentality." To be consistent with Taguchi, we want characteristics to be consistently close to the nominal. This is where we can useSPCs to measure how well we are doing.

Supplier Management – or – Choose Your Own Adventure

Life is an adventure. But as the late, great Neil Peart, drummer and lyricist for the best band ever, once wrote: "Adventures suck when you're having them," or something to that effect. It's only in retrospect that you can look back with pride and satisfaction on what you achieved during difficult times. With that in mind, we all recognize that the world of supplier management is a never-ending roller coaster ride of excitement, so I thought I would illustrate some of the AS6500 best practices principles through the respected literary device of the choose-your-own-adventure story. Have fun and good luck!

1. You are the Production Manager at Ace Aircraft Company and are responsible for the entire final assembly line. The contract your company has with the customer requires you to deliver one aircraft every three days. Your day started just fine because, in your mind, you are running the perfect factory. You have implemented all the practices from AS6500 (or so you think) and life is good. But as you are finishing your morning cup of coffee and donut, your Production Supervisor for the fuselage subassembly line shuffles into your office with a downtrodden face. He says, "Boss, we have a problem. Those access panel doors that cover Avionics Bay 2 aren't fitting. We've got dozens of them stacked up. We're trying to mix and match, but it's taking forever and some of them don't fit anywhere."

   You trust your Production Supervisor and have every confidence that he can take care of this. But it seems this must have been going on for a while if there are so many parts stacked up.

   If you decide to go out on the line to investigate for yourself, go to #2. If you decide to ignore it and let your production supervisor handle it, go to #3.

2. You follow your Production Supervisor out to the line. The problem hits you immediately – you can't believe you didn't see this coming sooner. Parts are piling up everywhere. The delivery containers for the access doors are scattered around the floor and every available shelf space. Parts are sitting in the containers, on the workbenches that surround the assembly station, and on the material shelves. It's chaos! You step back out to the main aisle to look at the metrics posted on the bulletin board and see they are falling behind schedule. It's a negative trend and it's getting worse.

   If you are beginning to feel overwhelmed, go to #4. If you choose to continue to investigate, go to #5.

3. You tell your Production Supervisor, "Thank you very much for bringing this to my attention. I'm sure you've got this. Let me know if you need any help." You dismiss him with a nod. You sit back down at your desk to think. This

can't really be that big of a deal, right? It's just the normal challenge of building a complex product. Someone is sure to sort it out – the supervisor, the quality department, the supplier management organization, the engineers – right? But the supervisor seemed more concerned than usual. And you're not sure you have confidence in those other departments. In fact, this could be the start of something very bad. Maybe it is time to do something after all. With resolute determination, you swivel your chair around to face your computer, open your personal folder, pull up your resume, and begin to update it. Time to find a new job. **THE END**.

4. The situation on the shop floor looks really bad. You go back to your office, shut the door, and weep. Once you pull yourself together, you sit down at your computer, open your personal folder, pull up your resume, and begin to update it, being sure to leave off any mention of managing this particular production line. You hope some company is desperate for a production manager and they won't bother checking references. **THE END**.

5. You go back to your office and pull up the data from the latest production metrics. You spend an hour looking through them and the supporting raw data from the shop floor control system. You end up taking a look through the Engineering folders and then at the files from Supplier Management. The dim light in your mind glows brighter in your mind as you realize the extent of the problem and some of the potential causes. You don't know exactly what went wrong, but you have some suspicions. You conclude that there are several organizations you need to visit.

   If you choose to visit Engineering, go to #6. If you choose to visit Supplier Management, go to #7. If you choose to visit the Program Manager, go to #8.

6. You walk down the hall towards Engineering, wishing you had a sword, shield, and chain mail armor. They are your constant nemesis. It's always a battle between your department and the engineers. You walk through their hallowed halls looking at the signs overhead for the Integrated Product Team responsible for the structure of the avionics bay. You spot the sign hanging from the ceiling that says, "Structures—Forward Fuselage—Avionics Bays." You certainly don't know everyone who works here, so you make your way to the boss box that has a nametag on the outside wall that says, "Nate Grombocher, Structures Engineer." As you approach his door, you see that his back is to you.

   If you challenge him to a duel to the death, go to #9. If you knock politely to have a discussion, go to #10.

7. As you enter the Supplier Management organization, you pass through their hospitality area with its well-stocked bar, overstuffed leather chairs, and tall bar tables suitable for hobnobbing around with supplier CEOs. You look for the department responsible for managing structural part suppliers.
   You decide to ask the secretary and she directs you to the office of Dan Martini. You introduce yourself and explain your problem. "What's up with our supplier of access panels for avionics bay 2? We're having a lot of quality problems and they won't fit."

   "Oh, them?" Dan replies. "That's Fred's Autobody and Aerospace Structures Technologies. They're a good company. I'll make a phone call and get it all straightened out. No worries. It'll be fixed on the next shipment."

If you are satisfied with his response, go to #13. If you want to dig a little deeper, go to #14.

8. You walk into the mahogany-lined corridors of the program management front office. You approach the secretary with trepidation and ask if his highness, George King, the program manager, might have a few minutes to spare. She rolls her eyes, looks at the calendar on the computer, and can't seem to come up with an excuse right away, so she allows you to pass into George's office. George is ensconced in a large, red leather chair behind an imposing wooden desk that may have sailed aboard the HMS Victory. A flicker of suspicion crosses his face but is soon replaced by his game face. "Welcome, what can I do for you?" You explain the issue.

    "Hmm, yes, it sounds like our supplier, Fred's Autobody and Aerospace Structures Technologies, maybe giving you some problems."

    "If I may ask, how did we choose them?"

    George pauses for a moment, seemingly trying to decide how much to tell you. "You see, we have certain …goals… that we program managers must achieve every year to meet our corporate targets. Fred and his company help us to achieve those goals."

    You want to say, "You mean the goal of poor quality and late deliveries?" but you hold your tongue. Instead, you ask, "What goals are those?"

    Once again, George pauses. "There are cost reduction goals we must achieve to keep our stockholders happy and to maintain our competitiveness in the industry. Surely you understand that?"

    "Yes, I suppose I do. So, what you're saying is that you went with Fred's Autobody and Aerospace Structures Technologies to save money?"

    "Yes, that's exactly what I'm saying. I'm glad you understand."

    Now you pause to decide how much to press. "If I may, how much money are we saving with Fred?"

    "I'm proud to say we're saving $1.98 on each and every part that they supply to us."

    If you decide to have an emotional outburst, go to #15. If you restrain yourself, go to #16.

9. You loudly announce, "Nate Grombacher, I hereby challenge you to a duel to the death! I'm sure that somehow you, your people, and your poor design for the access panel have caused me and my organization great anguish! Now stand and face me and fight like a man. Nate turns and you are not surprised to see that he is wearing the eldritch robes of a dark lord. You raise your sword to charge him when a phone rings and startles you out of your fantasy.

    Go to #10.

10. You knock on his door while at the same time saying, "Knock, knock." Nate turns around and you introduce yourself and explain the issue that has brought you here. Nate, who seems like a nice enough person, ponders for a moment. "Hmmm. Yes, there was some issue with that access panel. I don't remember exactly what it was, though. Let me take a look." He turns to his computer and spends a few moments clicking through folders. "Ah, here it is. Yeah, we went back and did a tolerance stack-up analysis and realized there

could be some mating issues, so we made a few changes. But it should be fixed. I don't know why you're still seeing problems."

If you are satisfied with his response, go to #11. If you pursue the discussion further, go to #12.

11. "Ok, thank you, Nate," you say as you leave his office and go back to yours. "Well, I'm glad I got that all figured out. Like he said, it should all be fixed. This must just be some temporary issue or some old parts they still have out in the factory. They'll work through it." You sit in your chair and lean back in blissful ignorance. Three weeks later, when your company has missed all of its contractual deliveries, your Vice President of Operations storms into your office, breaking your naïve serenity and says, "You're fired!" **THE END**.

12. "I hear what you're saying, Nate, but I don't know why we're still seeing parts that aren't fitting." He sits and thinks for a moment and then says, "I don't know either. We gave the new specs to…" His voice trails off. "Just a minute. Let me look at something else." He turns back to his computer and clicks through multiple screens (which seem to take forever to load.) "Yep, here it is. Here's the latest purchase order for the supplier. It still has the old drawing attached to it. For some reason, our changes never got flowed down."

    "That explains a lot," you reply. You stand there and wonder whose fault it is. Did Engineering not provide the new data package to Supplier Management? Did Supplier Management drop the ball? Was there some issue with your enterprise network where something just didn't get loaded correctly? At least you now have a good idea of what the problem is. "Thanks, Nate, I'll go look into it."

If you go to the Supplier Management organization, go to #7. If you go see the program manager, go to #8.

13. "Ok, thanks, Dan." You return to your office, confident that next week's shipment will be just fine. It's not. You're fired. **THE END**.

14. "I don't know, Dan. I'd like to find out a little bit more about this supplier, Fred's Autobody and Aerospace Structures Technologies. How are they doing? What are their capabilities?"

    Dan replies, "I actually don't have very much data on them. Mainly because they're an FOB-owned business."

    "An FOB-owned business? What's that?"

    "Well, you've heard of small businesses and women-owned businesses and minority-owned businesses, right? We have corporate incentives for contracting with those types of companies. But this is an FOB-owned business—a Friend of the Boss owned business. We have, uh, incentives for contracting with them, too."

    "That doesn't sound right."

    "Oh, it's fine. We still make sure they can do the work before we award them a contract and we keep tabs on them to make sure they're doing OK."

    "Since you've been 'keeping tabs,' what have you been finding with this FOB-owned company?"

Dan turns to check his computer. "Look at this, their on-time delivery is 100%! See, you can hardly get a good performance like this from your average supplier. I guess we're doing pretty good, huh?"

You offer a non-committal grunt. "What about their quality? That's what we're having problems with."

"Looks like that's fine, too. Our source inspectors report 98% first-pass yield. I don't know what you're complaining about. Fred's Autobody and Aerospace Structures Technologies sure seems to be doing well from where I sit."

"I guess I understand a little better now. I'll go do some more investigating and get back with you if I need anything."

"No problem, buddy. Hey, feel free to take one of those little bottles of airplane alcohol with you on the way out."

You leave (without taking the alcohol).

If you choose to visit Engineering, go to #6. If you choose to visit the Program Manager, go to #8.

15. When the program manager, George King, tells you that all the pain and extra work that your people are dealing with is just to save $1.98 per part, your head explodes. This saves the company the effort of firing you. **THE END**.

16. You manage to restrain yourself when the program manager, George King, tells you that all the pain and extra work that your people are dealing with is just to save $1.98 per part. "I see."

"Good. I knew you would understand. Is that all?"

If that is all, go to #17. If you want to ask for more, go to #18.

17. "Yes, that's all." You return to your office. Nothing ever gets better. You get fired. **THE END**.

18. As you turn to leave, you have an idea. "How about I make a trip to Fred's Autobody and Aerospace Structures Technologies. I can take a look around, talk to them about the issues we're having, and maybe get this resolved."

"Ewww. I don't know. That's going to cost money to send you there. And we've got a Supplier Management organization to manage our suppliers. I don't know if I want a loose cannon out there. Tell you what, why don't you just write a memo, send it to me, and I'll pass it along to Supplier Management?"

You decide to remain resolute because you know how this will end if you don't.

"No, I think I really need to go on-site. I could explain to them first-hand what we are seeing and help them to make some improvements."

George thinks about this for a moment.

"Very well. You may travel to see Fred. But just be careful not to make any constructive changes that they can charge us for!"

"Will do. Thank you."

Proceed to #19.

19. You arrive at Fred's Autobody and Aerospace Structures Technologies. It's about what you expected. A glorified garage that looks cluttered and old on the outside. You enter the lobby and the receptionist greets you and says that the owners will be right with you.

    Three men enter the lobby from the door behind the receptionist. The first man enthusiastically shakes your hand. "Hi, I'm Lawrence! This is my associate Curtiss and my other associate Maurice." The men are dressed in suits and ties, but there's something just a little bit off about them that you can't quite put your finger on.

    The one named Maurice says, "Let's go back to the little conference room."

    "No, you dummy, that one is too small," Curtis said. "This is an important man from our customer. We have to treat him with respect. We'll go to the big conference room."

    "No, you knuckleheads," said Lawrence. "The medium one is just right." They looked at each other and nodded. "Right this way."

    You follow them through the door, down the hallway, and into a nicely furnished, medium-sized conference room which is not too big and not too small.

    After everyone sits down, you say, "I suppose you know why I'm here. We've been having some problems with the parts that you've been shipping to us. So, I wanted to ask you about how you are controlling the quality of the parts. For example, did you perform a First Article Inspection on the first lot?"

    "First Article Inspection? First Article Inspection? Nah, we didn't do that," said Curtiss.

    Lawrence leaned over and whacked him on the side of the head. "What do you mean you didn't do that? I thought you always did that, you dunderhead."

    Maurice launched himself at Lawrence and, to your great surprise, poked his index finger and middle finger directly into Lawrence's eyes. "Hey, don't be picking on Curtiss. Who died and put you in charge, eh?" Confusion began to ensure.

    You try to calm them down. "Guys! Guys! Forget it! OK, so you didn't do a First Article Inspection. So, tell me about your process controls. How do you ensure that every part meets the drawing tolerances?"

    Maurice jumped up and down. "Oh, oh! I know this one!" He reached into his suit jacket pocket and pulled out a magnifying glass. "I inspect them! Each and every one!" He held up the glass to his eye at just the right angle so you could see his giant eyeball.

    You are now wondering what you've gotten yourself into. You also wonder what your company has gotten itself into. You decide to try one last question. "I see. Uhm, so what does your Quality department do? How do they sign off on the quality of each part?"

    Lawrence replied, "Quality department? What Quality department?"

    "Your company's Quality department? You must have one, right?"

"We don't need no stinkin' Quality department! Curtiss here once read a book that said quality is free. So, why would we pay for that? What do you take us for? Simpletons?"

"I'm sure that wasn't exactly the message of that book, but that's neither here nor there." You sit for a moment and gather your thoughts. Where do you go from here?

© Cartoon Resource

"I admit we may have missed one or two of the regulations in the Green Building Code."

If you decide that you should try to work with this company to improve their processes, go to #20. If you decide there's nothing more you can do here, go to #21. If you decide to just quit your job and go work at a fast-food joint, then you can mercifully end the story now.

20. "Fellows, you know we're having some problems with your parts. Is there anything I can do to help you with improving your quality?"

"I don't know. I suppose it depends," said Lawrence.

"It depends on what?"

"It depends on if it's free advice or not. We're not made of money, you know."

"Oh, of course. My company and I would be glad to work with you at no cost. We all just want to see things get better."

Curtiss leaped up from his chair. "Well, then certainly we'd be glad to hear what you have to say."

"Thank you. Here's what I'm thinking. We should probably start with a Manufacturing Readiness Level Assessment to get a baseline understanding of where you're at and what the risks are. You're familiar with MRLs, right?"

This time, it was Maurice's turn to leap out of his chair. "Oh, yes! And we're an eleven!"

Curtiss made a fist and bopped the top of his head. "You bozo, the MRLs only go to ten."

"Yeah, but we're better than that." Maurice reached out and grabbed Curtiss's nose and twisted it between his first two fingers. Maurice let out a yowl as they continued to argue about being ten verses eleven.

You try to interject. "Guys! Guys! Stop! Forget it! We'll use the MRL matrix later to figure out where you are. And it does only go to ten." Curtiss looked at Maurice and said, "I told you so."

"Once we do the MRL assessment, that will give us a good road map of where to go. In addition, we should take a look at the drawings we flowed down to you and identify some key characteristics."

At the mention of key characteristics, all three of them began jumping, yelling, and complaining.

"We hate key characteristics!"

"No one does key characteristics!"

"They cost too much"

You try to restore order and, seeing that you will make no progress on key characteristics, move on to the next suggestion. "OK, guys, how about Statistical Process Control? Surely you're familiar with that and you've maybe done some on other projects?"

They calm down and take their seats. They look at each other and Lawrence seems to be elected to speak for them. "Yes, of course, we know about SPC. We're not backward Neanderthals, you know. But it's just not for us. You do know that we work in a low rate environment, right? So, we get a free pass. SPC doesn't apply to us."

You take a deep breath. You've heard this argument before and you know techniques that can be used in a low rate environment. But just maybe these guys aren't ready for it. You realize that you're getting nowhere and decide to head back home, never having even gotten the chance to meet Fred, the namesake of Fred's Autobody and Aerospace Structures Technologies.

Go to #21.

21. As you head back to your company, you know that Fred's Autobody and Aerospace Structures Technologies is hopeless, and you will never be able to get good parts from them. This leaves you with the unenviable position of having to convince the program manager and the supplier management organization that they need to find a new supplier.

If you decide to visit the program manager, go to #22. If you decide to visit the supplier management organization, go to #23.

22. Once back to your office, you decide to send an email to George King, the program manager, to summarize your experience at Fred's Autobody and Aerospace Structures Technologies and to tell him you need to find a new

supplier. You write the email and send it off to him. It will probably be a day or two before you hear back, and maybe even longer, since he won't like your idea and will try to ignore you. You are surprised then to hear the telltale ding of your email program telling you that you have mail. He has already responded. You open the message with hesitation wondering what it will be. To your surprise, the first line reads, "I agree that you have a point and we may need a new supplier." Wow! You are shocked that he has so easily and quickly agreed with you.

But wait, the message continues. "However, you must survive the three challenges before I will approve it. The first challenge is: Don't bring me problems, bring me solutions. Identify a new supplier." Find a new supplier? That's not your job! That's the job of the Supplier Management organization.

If you choose to meet with Supplier Management, go to #24.
If you decide to ask around for help, go to #25.

23. You walk down to the Supplier Management organization to see Dan Martini.

"Dan! Hey, we need to talk about getting rid of Fred's Autobody and Aerospace Structures Technologies. I went to visit them and they're hopeless." You tell him all that you observed when you were there.

"Oh, I don't know about that. We have a long-term purchasing agreement with them. I can't just cancel that. There will be penalties and paperwork and more paperwork. That's a lot of work for my organization. "

"But they are killing production! If we don't change now, we will be the ones in violation of our contract with our customer."

"That sounds bad, but we have processes here that we have to follow. In fact, I don't even have the authority to switch suppliers."

"Who does?" As soon as you ask the question, you know the answer and a sudden feeling of fear develops in the pit of your stomach.

"Why, the Program Manager, of course. George King. You'll have to go see him to get that kind of approval."

George King. They tyrannical PM whose name strikes fear into the heart of his underlings. It will not be easy.

Go to #22.

24. You trek back to Dan Martini's office in Supplier Management and explain what you are trying to do. "Oh, finding a new supplier will be easy. It's getting them approved by the program manager that will be hard," he said. "See here. All I have to do is look through our database to find which suppliers are approved for that part." He clicks through some screens and frowns. "Unfortunately, the company that used to make that part for us went out of business after we pulled our work out of there. Hmmm. There's no one else in the system. Sorry about that."

"You mean that's it? There's no one else? It's not that difficult of a part. Surely, there are companies that do similar types of machining and processing?"

"I'm sure there are, it's just that our system isn't set up to search like that. I hear that the new version of our database may be able to do it and it should be installed next year. So, if you could hang on until then… After all, we don't want to get blamed for picking a bad supplier. But if you can find a company on your own, we can go through the process of adding them. I'm sorry, but you're on your own."

You say thank you and return to your office.

Go to #25.

25. Since it's up to you to find a new supplier, you realize that you need to call on many of the people you've networked with through the years at all of those conferences and professional committees (thank you, SAE International!) You open your desk drawer and sort through the many business cards you've gathered. You look through your old email contacts. You look at attendance lists from conferences and committees you've served on. Good thing you're such a networker!

You compose an email outlining your situation and the basic capabilities you need a supplier to have. You send it to each of the people who might have a lead on a good supplier. Now you sit back and wait.

The next day, your inbox is filled with emails with helpful suggestions. You follow up with the most promising ones and, after several days of emailing, phone calls, and research, you feel confident that you have several promising candidate suppliers. Now you're ready for the second challenge.

Go to #26.

26. You open the email from the program manager and read the second challenge. It says, "Don't endanger my annual bonus. The new supplier must contribute to my cost reduction goal." You sit back and ponder how you will meet this challenge. You realize this shouldn't actually be too hard. You can assume the new supplier will be approximately the cost of the old supplier (the one before Fred's Autobody and Aerospace Structures Technologies). And you can easily get the data from your Enterprise Resource Planning system on the manhours your team has spent trying to make the defective parts work. As you look through the data, you see it is already starting to show a big spike in touch labor costs. Chances are, you'd have to explain those increases anyway during the next staff meeting, so now you can use the cost increases to accomplish your mission. So, it looks like you've got a pretty airtight Return on Investment calculation! Now onto the third, final, and most difficult challenge.

Go to #27.

27. The third challenge reads, "You must make it through my secretary if you are to present the results of your first two challenges to me. Email is not satisfactory. You must convince my secretary to schedule a meeting of my valuable time with the likes of you." Mr. King's secretary, Donna Hassle, was indeed intimidating. Lesser men had forgone important meetings with Mr. King because she was so daunting. If she didn't like you, she could make your life miserable. So, how to get past her? You sit and ponder and come up with three potential ideas: stealth, flowers, or food.

If you want to try stealth, go to #28. If you want to try flowers, go to #29. If you want to try the food, go to #30.

28. You walk down the hallway towards the front office but don't go through the majestic double doors to the reception area where Donna the Secretary lurks in her lair. You stand off to the side, observing the comings and goings of

people from the office. Donna never seems to take a break, but it's nearing lunchtime and you were hoping she would leave her desk to go to the breakroom to get her food. As lunchtime comes and goes, you can't believe she isn't eating.

Finally, she turns to George King's office to say, "George, I'll be eating lunch now." It's about time! Here she goes! Much to your dismay, she leans down to her lower desk drawer, removes a large bag, sets it on her desk, and begins pulling out food. Clearly, this isn't going to work. She probably never goes to the restroom, either.

You get an idea that's so desperate it just might work. You walk down the hall to the supply room and return with two handfuls of paper clips and binder clips. While keeping outside the front office door, you heave the clips into the far corner of the room where they make a loud clatter. Donna looks up quizzically towards the sound of the noise. She stands up and walks over to the corner. As she begins to look behind the chairs for the source of the noise, you take the opportunity to dash across the reception area to George's office. Just as you get to his door, you feel a cold, steely hand clutch your shoulder. "And just where do you think you're going?" Donna asks. Her speed was inhuman. You've been caught. Now you will never get to meet with George King. Sadly, it is **THE END**.

29. You decide to try the direct approach and turn on the charm. You arrive in the front office with a dozen red roses. "Donna! How are you today? My, that pantsuit looks fetching. I realized you do so much for me and my department, and I've never properly thanked you. So, I brought you these flowers as a small toke of my appreciation." She eyes you suspiciously, but takes the flowers and looks them over.

"What do you want?" asks with a growl. You can't tell if that's her normal tone or if she's on to your game.

"What do I want? Oh, nothing at all! I really just wanted to say thank you and let you know that we appreciate everything you do."

She seems to soften as she smells the flowers.

You turn to walk away but then pause at the door. "Oh, there is one small thing I forgot to ask about. Would it be OK if I got on Mr. King's calendar sometime in the next few days? It's nothing urgent."

She immediately sees through your ploy and fire burns from her eyes. "Get out!" she snarls. You are doomed. It is the end for you.

30. You decide to try to bribe Donna the secretary with food. The question is, chocolate or donuts? Which kind of person is she, you wonder? You make your choice, running out at lunchtime to procure the goods. You return to the front office and cautiously enter Donna's lair.

"Uhm, excuse me, Ms. Hassle? I was wondering if I could get on Mr. King's calendar?"

She slowly looks up from her work, eyes about to shoot darts at you. You quickly reveal the bag you had been holding behind you back and place it on her desk. She pauses in her fiery madness with a quizzical look. She slowly opens the bag, gazes inside at the chocolate candy bars and fresh donuts, and looks up at you with a slight smile. "Of course. In fact, I think Mr. King is available right now. I'll buzz him and you can go right on in."

Pleased that you have successfully overcome the third challenge, you enter Mr. King's office.

You present your information on the new, proposed supplier and the cost savings.

"Congratulations," he says. "You have met my three challenges. I hereby approve of your new supplier."

Congratulations! You win the supplier management challenge!

"What we really need in manufacturing is someone who has super powers."

© Cartoon Resource

What have we learned from this great adventure? That it's easy to make fun of penny-pinching program managers, officious secretaries, and three-martini-lunch supplier managers? Yes, we have learned those things. But we've also learned how important suppliers are to the success of YOUR factory. We've also learned the importance of choosing the right supplier and that you should probably never choose a supplier with a name like Fred's Autobody and Aerospace Structures Technologies. We also learned it's important to flow down the right requirements to suppliers: Current designs, first article inspections, process controls, and Manufacturing Readiness Level assessments.

This is another area where AS6500 can lead to everlasting happiness. If only the entire organization in this adventure had been on board with its practices, your life in this fictional adventure would have been so much easier. Just like your real-life adventures in your job will be so much easier if only everyone would just follow AS6500!

When you try to get other organizations to implement these best practices, don't you sometimes feel like a parent whose children won't listen? You have all this wisdom and no one follows it!

Maybe you could give the other managers a copy of this book. That way, they can see the error of their ways and be motivated to follow the best practices in the standard. But be sure to buy them their own copy, so I can get more royalties. And maybe white-out (do they still sell that stuff?) the offensive stuff about program managers and supplier managers.

Cybersecurity as It Relates to Manufacturing

Typically, Manufacturing and Quality Engineers run away from software issues. They just aren't in our wheelhouse. (I really hate that buzzword, but I feel obliged to use it since so much of our leadership uses it.) Add to that the complexities of computer networks and operating systems, and cybersecurity becomes something that we can justifiably claim ignorance of. And I can claim a lot of ignorance.

However…you knew this was coming, right?… There are some elements of cybersecurity that are in our wheelhouse. (There's that offensive word again.) Cybersecurity issues can certainly impact the manufacturing facility, tooling, and test equipment. We call these areas Operational Technologies and they are systems that deal with the physical transformation of products and services. In other words, operational technologies include software that controls equipment, such as tooling, test equipment, or inspection equipment. Information Technology, on the other hand, is what we traditionally think of as the software systems managed by the IT community—corporate systems, Enterprise Resource Planning systems, etc. For those systems, you can sleep soundly, knowing that your crack IT staff is all over that stuff. The OT systems, on the other hand, well, not so much. Those systems aren't very glamorous, and the software engineers didn't go to school to work on unglamorous, factory equipment. That means it's all up to you.

I am not an expert on cybersecurity, and I'm willing to bet you aren't either. I know nothing about firewalls and virus protection software except all of it seems to just make life harder. I do remember some FORTRAN, but that probably won't help much.

Having said that, there are a few basic things you can do to protect your perfect factory from the Chinese Intelligence Service, the disgruntled employee, and the evil teenage hacker living in his parent's basement. To illustrate some of the proper protection techniques, take the following quiz to identify the proper practices for Operational Technology cybersecurity:

1. The best place to locate computer servers is:

    ☑ a. In a secure, undisclosed location

    ☑ b. In the bathroom closet of a fly-by-night internet provider

    ☑ c. In the center of the factory so that everyone can keep an eye on them

2. Machine operators should be able to:

☑ a. Run the programs, but not make changes to the software

☑ b. Edit the software as they see fit

☑ c. Be able to watch funny cat videos on the interface screen of your new 5-axis milling machine

3. Everyone in the factory should be trained in:

☑ a. Best practices to safeguard Operational Technology Systems

☑ b. The finer points of C++, JAVA, Python, and Visual Basic

☑ c. How best to hotwire the lathe to work when the network is down

4. An example of a good password is:

☑ a. IluvAS6500!!!!!

☑ b. password

☑ c. sdlkfjo4o4h4iirjf94987654efg

5. A good cyber incident management system will include:

☑ a. Tracking of the identification, containment, corrective action, and preventive action for cyber incidents

☑ b. PowerPoint charts with incomprehensible details of system architectures

☑ c. Hacker of the month award

6. When screening new hires, it is important to:

☑ a. Perform a background check

☑ b. Not hire a guy named "Will Hackyu"

☑ c. Ask, "If you were a computer hacker, how would you hack our systems?"

If I need to include an answer key to tell you the correct answers, you are in worse shape than I thought and maybe you should just give up now and surrender the keys of your factory to Russian Oligarchs.

Following these simple practices won't keep your perfect factory safe, but it will keep you from looking dumb if you were the person that hired Mr. Will Hackyu.

CHAPTER 9

Conclusion

"What if we don't change at all ...
and something magical just happens?"

© Cartoon Resource

Let's put together everything you've learned. If you apply all these principles, the perfect factory is just around the corner, which is a metaphor for saying it will be here soon, not that the perfect factory is your competitor's facility that is just around the corner.

When you have a perfect factory, your life will also be perfect. Here is a short comparison of what your life will now be like, compared to those poor slobs still toiling away in those inefficient companies.

Poor slobs who manage poor slobby factories:

Live in constant stress

Tied to a pager on their hip 24/7

    Still have a pager because the company can't afford a cell phone

Yelled at by the CEO

Yelled at by customers

Yelled at by coworkers

Tires slashed by underlings

You:

The only time you are exhausted is when you have to walk the golf course because there are no carts available.

Rainbows appear in the sky above you. They end in the pot of gold that is in your bank account.

Fellow employees carry you in from the parking lot on their shoulders singing, "For he's a jolly good fellow."

Harvard Business Review devotes an entire issue to your success

60 Minutes devotes an entire episode to the failure of your competitor

A Final Note: Dispensing with the Checklist Mentality

AS6500 was written to provide an opportunity for improvement. Organizations can compare their current practices to the requirements in the standard and identify gaps. Manufacturing practitioners know what we need to do. We've all been taught the same techniques and approaches that improve efficiency and quality. The problem is, we don't always have the support of leadership or the resources to actually perform these best practices. But now, Manufacturing Managers can use AS6500 as a tool to communicate to leadership that these are industry-standard practices that must be used if we are to stay competitive with other companies and ensure on-budget and on-schedule quality deliveries. The standard can provide "top cover" for you to manage to help justify increased attention and resources in those gap areas that will result in improved performance.

With this purpose in mind, we must be careful to avoid the "checklist mentality." This is the mindset where an auditor looks at every single requirement and every jot and tittle of the standard and develops an exhaustive checklist to audit compliance. Every single requirement must be proven to be accomplished, usually with documented evidence. This approach misses the point of the standard.

Instead, auditors should work with the Manufacturing Managers to identify weak areas or areas of opportunity. Stand back and look at the common, repetitive problem areas and see if better manufacturing management practices could improve them. Consider the needs of the program and the manufacturing risks. Use AS6500 to bolster those areas by improving the processes and procedures for those weak areas and obtaining the budget to ensure they get accomplished.

Yes, you will probably have customers come in and audit you to the letter of the law. And you can show them a compliance matrix that maps the requirements of AS6500 to your existing processes and practices. But if they try to be hardcore auditors and get lost in the weeds, give them a copy of this book (and then buy yourself another copy) so they can understand your vision. Once they've read this finely written missive, they are sure to get on board with you.

Congratulations! You've made it through the book! Now you have all the know-how and tricks of the trade to run the perfect factory! Program Managers and Engineers from the Dark Side have no chance against you. You can do it! Now get out there and identify some key characteristics! Run some Process FMEAS! Manipulate those metrics to make you look like a genius. You are on the road to everlasting happiness through AS6500!

appendix: additional information of AS6500's relation to manufacturing readiness levels

MRLs in SAE AS6500

SAE AS6500, "Manufacturing Management Program," is a standard for requiring proven manufacturing management practices to deliver affordable and capable systems. It applies to all phases of a system acquisition life cycle and may be specified in a contract on any program with manufacturing content. This standard was created to implement manufacturing management practices aimed at promoting the timely development, production, modification, fielding, and sustainment of affordable products by addressing manufacturing issues throughout the program life cycle.

AS6500 was designed to be fully compatible with Manufacturing Readiness Levels. It is not required for successfully implementing MRLs. However, it may help decrease manufacturing risk by requiring the conduct of MRL assessments, the development of a manufacturing plan, and the implementation of other manufacturing best practices.

> For additional guidance on AS6500, refer to MIL-HDBK-896A, "Manufacturing Management Program Guide."

Requirements for Conducting MRL Assessments in AS6500

When imposed contractually, AS6500 requires the conduct of MRL assessments prior to major milestones and technical reviews. It also requires organizations to:

- Identify MRL targets
- Document manufacturing risks

- Include critical suppliers in MRL assessments
- Develop and implement manufacturing maturation and risk reduction plans for threads that are not at the target MRL

The standard encourages the use of MRL criteria to support Manufacturing Feasibility Assessments and Production Readiness Reviews.

Although the requirements for MRL assessments in AS6500 do not include all of the recommended Statement of Work elements in section 6.5, "SOW Language for Contracts," they do address many of them. If AS6500 is imposed contractually, the minimum requirements for MRL assessments would be adequately covered.

Requirements for a Manufacturing Plan in AS6500

Section 6.6 of this Deskbook, "Other Deliverables," discusses the option of including plans for implementing MRLs in a Manufacturing Plan. AS6500, Section 6.4, requires the organization to establish and maintain a Manufacturing Plan. The standard lists topics that must be addressed in the plan, including manufacturing technologies, producibility, facilities, tooling, etc. AS6500 does not specifically require the Manufacturing Plan to address MRLs, nor does it require the plan to be a deliverable document.

However, since many of the topics that must be addressed in the Manufacturing Plan per AS6500 correspond to MRL threads, it can be a useful source of information when conducting MRL assessments.

Requirements for Activities Related to MRL Threads in AS6500

The MRL matrix is a collection of criteria against which manufacturing maturity is measured. The criteria themselves do not contractually direct that certain activities be accomplished. AS6500 is a tasking document that requires many of those activities to be accomplished.

Using Key Characteristics (KCs) as an example, the criteria for MRL 6, Subthread B.2, Design Maturity, states that, "Preliminary design KCs have been identified…" The MRL matrix does not require a contractor to identify KCs. Rather, it is an expectation for what should take place, in this case, with respect to KCs prior to PDR. On the other hand, AS6500 specifically requires organizations to identify KCs in the Technical Data Package. If the requirements of AS6500 are implemented, then the criteria of MRL 6, Subthread B-2 should be satisfied.

TABLE A.1 Mapping of MRL Threads to AS6500 Requirements

MRL Thread	AS6500 Requirement
Technology and Industrial Base	6.4.1 Supply Chain and Material Management
	6.4.2 Manufacturing Technology Development
Design	6.2.1 Producibility Analysis
	6.2.1c Design Trade Studies
	6.2.2 Key Characteristics
	6.2.3 Process FMEAs
Cost & Funding	6.4.3 Cost
Materials	6.4.1 Supply Chain and Material Management
	6.5.8 Supplier Management
Process Capability & Control	6.4.4 Manufacturing Modeling & Simulation
	6.5.3 Continuous Improvement
	6.5.4 Process Control Plans
	6.5.5 Process Capabilities
Quality Management	6.3 Manufacturing Risk Identification
	6.5.2 Manufacturing Surveillance
	6.5.3 Continuous Improvement
	6.5.7 FAIs/FATs
	6.5.8 Supplier Management
	6.5.9 Supplier Quality
Manufacturing Workforce	6.4.6 Manufacturing Workforce
Facilities	6.4.7 Tooling/Test Equipment/Facilities
Manufacturing Management	6.4 Manufacturing Planning
	6.4.5 Manufacturing System Verification
	6.5.1 Production Scheduling and Control
	6.5.2 Manufacturing Surveillance

The activities required by AS6500 and the criteria in the MRL matrix are highly complementary (refer to Figure 6-1). While not every MRL criterion is covered, AS6500 requires activities that correspond to many of the topics addressed in the MRL threads. Ideally, if AS6500 is implemented effectively, then there is a high probability that the activities being assessed by the MRL criteria will have been accomplished and the product/process will successfully achieve the target MRL (Table A.1).

David Karr is the Technical Advisor for Manufacturing and Quality in the Engineering Services Directorate at the Air Force's Life Cycle Management Center at Wright-Patterson Air Force Base. He is responsible for developing policies and processes in the areas of manufacturing and quality for the Center and for providing manufacturing guidance to programs.

In his 30 years at AFLCMC, David has been assigned to the Maverick Missile, Tacit Rainbow, LANTIRN, F-22, and B-1 programs. As the Engineering staff's Technical Advisor, he provided support to the F-22, F-35, KC-46, JSTARS, the new B-21 Bomber, and numerous other programs.

Mr. Karr chairs the SAE International G-23 Committee for Manufacturing Management. Under his leadership, the committee developed and published the industry standard for manufacturing management, AS6500.

Despite being an engineer, David pretends to be a writer in his spare time. Every year, he writes his church's Christmas pageants, which include the usual angels, shepherds, wise men, and baby Jesus, but also incorporate such off-the-wall themes as a Star Wars/Star Trek mashup, a Get Smart take-off, and an adaptation of the Grinch Who Stole Christmas. His next goal is to write a Christmas pageant incorporating key elements of The Princess Bride.

EDUCATION

1987 Bachelor of Science, Electrical Engineering, Grove City College
1997 Master of Science, Engineering Management, University of Dayton
2001 Air War College

index

97

www.ingramcontent.com/pod-product-compliance
Lightning Source LLC
Chambersburg PA
CBHW040758220326
41597CB00029BB/4979